# THE SOCIAL CONSTRUCTION
# OF REFORM

# THE SOCIAL CONSTRUCTION
# OF REFORM

## Crime Prevention and
## Community Organizations

ST. JOSEPH'S UNIVERSITY

3 9353 00236 7298

Dan A. Lewis
Jane A. Grant
*and*
Dennis P. Rosenbaum

HV
7431
.L48
1988

Transaction Books
New Brunswick (USA) and Oxford (UK)

Copyright © 1988 by Transaction, Inc.
New Brunswick, New Jersey 08903

All rights reserved under International and Pan-American Copyright Conventions. No part of this book may be reproduced or transmitted in any
form or by any means, electronic or mechanical, including photocopy,
recording, or any information storage and retrieval system, without prior
permission in writing from the publisher. All inquiries should be addressed
to Transaction Books, Rutgers—The State University, New Brunswick,
New Jersey 08903.

Library of Congress Catalog Number: 87-4983
ISBN 0-88738-138-3
Printed in the United States of America

**Library of Congress Cataloging-in-Publication Data**

Lewis, Dan A.
    The social construction of reform, crime
prevention, and community organizations.

    Bibliography: p.
    Includes index.
    1. Crime prevention—Citizen participation—
Case studies.    2. Community organization—Case
studies.    I. Grant, Jane A.    II. Rosenbaum, Dennis P.
III. Title.
HV7431.L48    1987        364.4'0458        87-4983

# Contents

# List of Tables and Figures

# Acknowledgments

The funding for the research which is described in this book came from a generous grant from the Ford Foundation to Northwestern University. We are especially grateful to Sharon Rowser who was our project monitor at the foundation. The Center for Urban Affairs and Policy Research at Northwestern served as the home for the study and offered a variety of support as we transformed the research report into this book. Its director, Margaret T. Gordon, was her usual helpful self throughout all the stages of this project. Gale Hagan and Janet Soule did a wonderful job of typing the thousands of manuscript pages.

There are dozens of organizations which allowed us access to their premises and people. Without their help, the book, quite simply, could not have been written. While some of these people were none too happy with our discussion of their activities, we can only hope that they will find some merit in what we have had to say as they gain some distance from the period we are describing. We are particularly indebted to the Citizens Information Service for their kind help.

*A special note:* Chapter 2 was adapted from an earlier unpublished manuscript, *Money, Maintenance and Mission: The Effect of External Funding on Poor People's Community Organizations,* by Dan A. Lewis and Susan C. Clarke (1983).

Finally, it never goes without saying that the opinions in this book are those of the authors and do not represent the position of either Northwestern University or the Ford Foundation.

# 1

# Introduction

This book stands at the crossroads between criminology and social reform. It is a book about what happens when a crime prevention program is introduced into urban neighborhoods as a way of initiating change. It is a book about social theory and the use of "community" programs in reform efforts. And finally it is a book about social policy and its evaluation. We hope to shed some light on the interplay between organizations in our society and how reform efforts work. We argue that much of what passes for professional judgments about how nothing works is distorted by the way social reform is defined and depoliticized. Social reform is typically conceptualized as an exercise in the consumption of a new hierarchy of values, that is, as an attempt by a coalition of interests to change the way we go about distributing resources in our society. We see social reform as *collective action* in which groups pursue political ends at the same time they accommodate each other.

Thus, reform is not an idea we implement; rather reform is something produced by the interactions between groups, which comes to have meaning through interpretations by social institutions. How those interpretations are produced is an equally important topic which will be indirectly addressed here. Social reforms are produced by a sequence of interactions between people working within and between organizations and then working through relationships in which competing agendas lead to conflict and compromise.

More attention ought to be paid to the organizations in subordinate positions in the reform process. This reorientation would permit a better understanding of the reforms we are interested in and perhaps offer new criteria with which to assess effectiveness. We see our work as giving meaning to the experience of subordinate groups, not only because our political sympathies lie with them, but also because it is only when we come to understand their activities *through their eyes* that we will make any headway assessing outcomes. Failure, like beauty, is in the eye of the beholder.

1

While this approach is hardly new, it is rarely used to assess "dilemmas of social reform." It is typically used to assess what happens *within* organizations, especially those concerned with deviance and its control (Becker, 1963). But organizations also stand in a hierarchy with respect to one another. Indeed, how organizations see themselves, and the effectiveness of their activity, depends in large measure on the vantage point from which they participate in the reform effort. There is in social reform, as in other areas of social life, a "hierarchy of credibility" (Becker, 1967), which dictates whom we are supposed to believe about what is going on and whose view of the activity is worthwhile. It is that hierarchy we seek to challenge, with the hope that the view from below increases our understanding.

Both liberal and conservative scholars have assumed away the key question we face in social reform efforts, namely, how much attention is paid to the goals of reformers and what factors account for the lack of consensus about goals and purposes. In this study, we examine how the interests of a major foundation, a metropolitan reform group, several community organizations and many local residents interacted to produce something called "community crime prevention" and how the competing interests and ideologies of these groups and individuals resulted in the reform effort, an effort which was a political success for most of the organizations involved but had little influence on local residents and was only peripherally about crime prevention.

What we saw and will discuss in detail are people in organizations accommodating themselves to each other, acting together in ways which met the expectations of others while preserving their own interests. This observation suggests that the role of national elites is limited in the changing of basic social and economic relations in communities. Rather those relations shape what the reform becomes. Social reform is an interactive process in which the interests and needs of those who seek reform, and those who are the targets of reform, have to be taken much more seriously if we are to understand the results. Scholars too often adopt the same hierarchy of values that is proposed by the reform entrepreneurs they are studying. The issue before the reformers is to convince those participating in the effort that they should internalize those values. The issue before the researcher then is to chart that internalization process and discuss the ways that it fell short, suggesting that those who implement future reform efforts need more expertise, money or commitment to avoid "failure." For us, the issue is to chart the interactions between actors and organizations and to analyze how their differing ideologies and interests shaped the way they went about the reform business, and how organizations accommodated to others.

We see social reform as *collective action,* that is, as the interactions between people which shape mutual accommodations, over the definition of social problems. Park (1921) suggested that the shape of that action depends upon the *social groups* which are involved in the reform. If we are to understand the process which produces the reform we must look to the purposes of the social groups involved.

> Every such society or social group, even the most ephemeral, will ordinarily have (a) some relatively formal method of defining its aim and formulating its policies, making them explicit, and (b) some machinery, functionary, or other arrangement for realizing its aim and carrying its policies into effect (p. 171).

Park calls the groups involved in this activity "conflict and accommodation groups" and their adaptation to each other creates the political realm. Following Blumer (1971) we can say that reform efforts are part of the process of groups collectively defining social problems, usually implementing an official plan which defines who does what about the problem. A social reform is that part of the definition process in which action is taken to improve the problem in question with competing groups shaping what transpires. People adjust to the needs of others and the results may be at odds with the formal goals of some of those involved in the process. Governments and foundations participate in a process they would rather control. Our definition emphasizes the importance of process, of the continuing give and take of people accommodating themselves to others over time within groups.

What social scientists have seen as the failure of many social reforms and policies may be more the failure of those social scientists to conceptualize an approach to the study of these issues which can capture the complexities of collective behavior. Perhaps our social scientists have failed rather than our policies. They have failed to see organizations in conflict. In pursuing the interests of the government and in undervaluing the needs and experiences of the people who are affected by the reforms, they have legitimized state concerns at the expense of the conflicts involved. The lack of governmental authority in our society is not an outcome to bemoan, but rather a condition to weave into our approach to studying reform. The federal government, much less national foundations, has limited authority to dictate what local units of government and community organizations must do. Bureaucracies have difficulty achieving their ends because of the lack of authority that its leaders have and their inability to produce compliance among subordinates. Citizens see themselves as free to choose which government directives to follow. An emphasis on individualism, freedom, and limited government in our political culture make consensus on outcomes difficult to produce. A central research issue is to show how this state of affairs shapes reform efforts and with what effect.

Our faith in the capacity of the government to improve the lives of citizens through concerted action has been shaken by this mistaken assumption of government authority. American governmental institutions have always had trouble preserving their authority. We have seen the formation of a new consensus about the limitations and ironies of trying to help, and we are left with a reliance on markets and charity as the way to proceed, precisely because we have not taken this lack of authority seriously. The new consensus emerges from two sources. The first and most obvious are the talented group of conservative scholars and analysts who have written well about how the liberal policies and reforms implemented have had the opposite effect from the ones their proponents suggest. Where the liberal entrepreneurs of the last twenty–five years saw reform as the answer to problems created by the economy and the society, these men see the policies themselves as creating the incentives for deviant and criminal behavior. The other source of this sea change were the liberal social scientists who concluded that "nothing works" or at least not very well. Whether this judgment was due to methodological or ideological blinders will be debated for some time to come, but the result was something akin to Rossi's Iron Law (1978) which states that "the expected value for any measured effect of a social program is zero." Liberal social scientists could find little impact. Conservatives were saying that the policies themselves were the problem. And all this in a period when the mounting federal deficit dictated frugality.

Liberals say we have failed at reform because of the intransigence of the problems we face and the weak interventions we have at our disposal (Haveman, 1977). Conservatives argue that government is too powerful and rewards the very behaviors it seeks to change. In the former scenario the reformers are too weak and in the latter they are too strong, but in both cases social reforms are treated as independent activities which are separate and distinguishable from the society they impact. Liberals bemoan the lack of solutions to social problems, while a more recent crop of conservatives emphasizes how the reformers actually produce the problems they were meant to solve. While both approaches make a contribution to our understanding of reform, they both underestimate the interactive aspects of the reform process. Both liberals and conservatives assume an authoritative role for the reformer. Liberals are confused when that authority does not translate into successful outcomes and conservatives denounce these efforts as too authoritative producing the very behaviors they were meant to obliterate. Both traditions assume away the very issues which lie at the heart of the current dilemma, namely, the interactive nature of authority in our society.

Marris and Rein (1967) suggest why this "collective action" approach is so applicable to the United States. The federal system, the importance of democratic norms and the dispersal of power among many different elites create an environment for action in which voluntary compliance is essential for social reform. Coercion by the government or a powerful private organization is not a useful way to bring groups together to change the distribution of power because coercion brings resistance. The compliance it may induce will be formal and halfhearted and will not lead to the changes sought by the reform entrepreneurs. Thus in most reform efforts many different organizations must be committed to the effort if it is to have a chance of success and that means each must find a reason for participation which enhances its own goals and interests.

This problem is compounded when community organizations are involved in the reform effort, for all community groups must solve the problem of their own maintenance. This not only involves recruiting people to join the group, but also finding the resources that will keep the group going. Sometimes the tasks can be completed through the recruitment of those with sufficient resources to give, but most often recruitment and maintenance are two separate tasks. Community organizations find ways to survive. They do this in accordance with the cultures that have emerged within the groups over time.

Community groups also have missions, that is, goals they seek to achieve and political changes they pursue. The groups we studied all took as their mandate the exercise of control over the local area; by that, we mean they sought to shape the nature of the community in terms of the activities that took place and how their turf was used. Community organizations seek to shape the character of the area they purport to represent. To do this they must articulate the issues that will attract members and achieve the objectives those individuals find compelling. We refer to this capacity as political development.

On September 16, 1982 the Citizens Information Service of Illinois (CIS) was awarded a grant of $200,000 from the Ford Foundation. The next year, CIS received $350,000 from Ford. The grants were awarded to the organization so that it could continue its work in the area of community crime prevention for one year. For seventeen months prior to the award, CIS had been administering a government grant that supported the work of a coalition of groups to prevent crime at the neighborhood level. The Ford grant extended the capacity of the groups to continue the activity. What follows is our analysis of the activities of the groups as they used the Ford funding to prevent crime.

Community organizations seek to maintain themselves and develop politically. Organizational cultures emerge to solve these problems of maintenance, and both define and reflect missions. How they do crime prevention is a derivative of this culture and maintenance needs. Organizational context can shape a crime prevention program in profound ways. The Ford Foundation project has meaning for the community organizations within the cultural context of the groups that participated. It also has meaning in the context of the national culture which spawned the funding. While the meaning the groups attached to what they do is important in its own right, it is also desperately important from the point of view of the observer, for it determines literally how the groups define the situation and ultimately what they do.

Elmore (1979) suggests that the individuals who are the targets of the reform also must have a reason for participating in the effort and altering their behavior. He adds that the interaction between the administrative unit charged with reforming the person and the person him or herself will combine with respect to success. At this intersection, there are differences of culture, self–interest and politics which affect how a reform effort goes. It is an interaction in which both parties have considerable power to shape the outcomes both by how they participate and how they avoid that participation.

People who are engaged in social reform act with an eye to the responses of others involved in that action. Often we see that actors disagree over the correct way to define much less pursue the reform and the contingencies of both organizational and political life force compromises about how to proceed. Reforms happen between people and people bring to those interactions a set of interests and purposes which shape how they relate to others. While some of those interests precede the interaction there are also accommodations that occur between the actors to adjust one's own actions to the actions of others, and to mutual expectations.

The result of all this adjustment and compromise is that reform is about a lot of people acting together, often at cross purposes, but always with an eye to how others involved will react to what they do. If this is the case, studies of social reforms which focus only on the goals and ideas of legislators and intellectuals will miss the importance of the interaction between actors and organizations which pursue the reform. While the reform effort is usually defined and endorsed by elites, it also must be "implemented" through many organizations and individuals. It is the mutual accommodation between these groups which creates the reform and not the least of these are those whom the effort would seek to change. Thus, reform, rather than being a rule or goal guiding political life, turns out to be an achievement, a social product that is constructed through collective actions which in themselves have multiple origins and goals (Brown, 1978). It is the purpose of this book to analyze how one such product was created by the collective action of groups and individuals who sought to accommodate themselves to each other over an urban crime prevention program. We hope to demonstrate how reforms require the overt or tacit cooperation of many people and groups. Failure and success in this approach are not the consequences of poor thinking on the part of reform entrepreneurs or the lack of resources. Rather, they are the products of collective action, and assessments of that product emerge from and through that same collective action. Reforms are not official plans. They are the definitions and evaluations of such plans by groups. Thus, reform is not the *origin* of collective action, but rather the *result.*

As recent studies of the implementation process have made obvious, reform efforts include a variety of groups and organizations working together. In the case of the research which we will discuss in this book, there are four levels at which collective action takes place between groups and actors. They can be typed as relations between funder and grantee, coordinating unit and implementation units, within the implementation units and between these units and the targets of change. At each level, people interact in face to face ways as well as on paper and the result of those interactions produces the reform. Elmore (1979) suggests that the most important level for social reforms is the last in which an administrative unit tries to alter the behavior of citizens. A great deal of what goes into this contact depends on the mutual accommodation process which precedes this activity. What is missing in the work of those who study this phenomenon is the lack of attention to the interests and goals of those who are to be changed. While criminology is filled with discussions of the recalcitrance of criminals and other deviants to personal redemption, these discussions are rarely linked to the literature which studies the reform process itself. We will try to remedy this situation.

If social reform is collective action, it is action around ideas about how to improve life. Much of the accommodation process revolves around how to interpret and implement ideas about doing things differently, while enhancing the group's position and resources. Indeed, social reform usually identifies some aspect of community life which has appeared to some to be a problem. In the study with which this book is concerned, that problem is crime and the solution focused on strengthening communities. How ideas about what to do are shared and what individuals in different groups do with those ideas are the ingredients of collective action, but that action clearly revolves around a set of propositions about the crime problem and how "community programs" solve it. The sources of these ideas and their roles in groups will be one of the focuses of this book. Often in the study of social reform the ideas which supposedly guide the reform are celebrated rather than analyzed. Too often, the scholars who study these reform efforts share the same ideology with the reformers they seek to understand

and thus reproduce the reform mentality in their scholarship, taking the reformer's intentions at face value and treating disappointing results as surprising and due to the intransigence of a complicated and often mean-spirited society.

What needs to be elaborated is how these ideas about community work in the interactive settings described earlier. As Cohen (1985) points out, community initiatives have been treated as an alternative to the conventional solutions to problems of social control. They might be better seen as supplements to the status quo, using the ideological institution of community to make minor calibrations appear as the fundamental change.

In this book, we will analyze the "implementation" of the grant by the groups involved. We will do this by first describing the origins of the intervention the groups committed themselves to doing, (what is called community crime prevention) and look at the impact of external funding on community organizations as a generic issue. We approach our task with the proposition that the external support has important effects on the groups in general; and to understand how the money for crime prevention will be used we must first come to terms with the general issue of outside funding of community organizations. After these introductory chapters, we will take a careful look at what the groups did with the Foundation's support and offer a perspective for understanding their approach. We argue that the political development of the group will determine how the external funds will be used, that those funds are neither a positive nor a negative in themselves, but that they take their meaning from the politics of the group that receives them. Thus, to grasp how well the groups implemented crime prevention is to first determine the political culture of the group and how the particular crime prevention strategy employed supports that approach. Finally, we take a close look at "block watch" as the tactic most often employed by the groups, or more precisely the tactic the groups said they would use if they were funded. We end with some thoughts on "community" programs and their ideological foundations.

# 2

# Pragmatic Interactionism and Reform

In this chapter, we want to set the conceptual framework for the discussion which will follow. To do that, we need to expand our introductory remarks into a specific approach to the material that will be presented later in the book. We will call our approach *pragmatic interactionism,* with the hope that this term will evoke a notion of self–interested accommodation between both individuals and groups. We make a distinction between our approach and symbolic interactionism which focuses on how the interaction between people produces self concepts and social constructions or meanings for situations. We see interactional analysis as absolutely essential, but in a *regulative* rather than *constitutive* way. We do not know how selves and situations are constructed in social policy contexts and leave to others this difficult theoretical task, but we do think that interactions between groups and individuals regulate what we do and how we set goals, especially when it comes to political and economic situations.

Much of the work in sociology which is related to social policy and reform has focused on social problems, either their magnitude in the natural world, or their construction in a social world. Within the latter tradition, the influence of the Chicago School and its symbolic interactionist wing has led to an intense interest in how the social problems themselves are "created" by those who make and enforce rules. While this line of work has led to important theoretical contributions, it has not led to work on how these definitions are related to the actual workings of policies and programs meant to reduce or eliminate the problem in question. We have come to understand how people are recruited to fill the social problem category (e.g., delinquent, mental patient, alcoholic, etc.), but we know little about interactions between actors once the category has been created. The pragmatic interactionist perspective focuses less on the creation of categories and more on the interactions which occur between those who fill those categories. Very often the reform efforts which surround the social problem involve the activities of many people beyond the deviant class.

9

The focus on the creation of the social problem and the deviant self leaves unasked many questions about the how the efforts to improve the situation evolve politically and socially.

With this in mind, we will set the framework for this study. As we suggested in the introduction, there are related levels on which interactions around reform take place. These result in accommodations between groups, when individuals representing the interests of groups which employ them, or with which they identify, reach an accommodation about some area of mutual interest. Interactions at each level set the tone for further developments at other levels, by shaping issues which must be dealt with or by agreeing to implement activities at those other levels. There is much in the political science literature on these interactions between units of government (implementation and intergovernmental relations) and there is some discussion of these interactions between government units and community organizations and protest groups. Since our interest is in community organizations in the reform process, we will begin by looking carefully at how community groups accommodate themselves to funding agencies which support their activities. The negotiations between the community groups and these external funders (foundations and government agencies) are the first level of interaction.

Concerted efforts to redistribute power and resources, at least since World War II, have begun less with directly political strategies aimed at legislation and more through projects and programs which seek to demonstrate the benefits of reform (Moynihan, 1965). These efforts have to be supported by elite institutions. We begin here because each reform effort in this study has had a grant or contract in its early life to support these activities. This "professionalization of reform" suggests that the interests and goals of funding agencies must be squared with the interests and goals of those who will carry out the projects. It is here then that a study of reform must begin, for it is here that the first set of negotiations takes place between those who wish to fund a particular reform and those who seek funds. While there has been some work in this area, it often defines away the importance of the interactions by assuming that any elite support cannot be in the interest of the community or else it would not have been given in the first place (Gittell, 1980). By looking at the benefits and costs which accrue to the group, we can take this discussion one step further, seeing when groups advance their interests when they take outside funding and when they do not.

There are some who believe that community groups cannot benefit from outside funding of their efforts, while others take it as self–evident that outside support helps a group achieve its goals precisely because the goals of funders and community groups are assumed to be convergent. In the first, real social reform cannot happen and in the latter reform is a matter of incremental change. However, if the accommodation process is the key to how reforms proceed, then neither perspective is adequate, for they do not specify the conditions under which the reform effort succeeds or fails. What is needed is an approach to this level of interaction between funders and community groups which specifies the conditions under which the groups achieve what they want.

Sociologists should be aware of the limits of the paradigms they use. Critics from within and outside of the discipline have identified the tendency to dismiss rationality among actors and to see the person as determined by the institutions and roles in which he is ensconced (Piven, 1981). Often sociologists treat social relations as if the state and legitimate violence did not exist. These tendencies have led to a determinism or structuralism which treats the actor as a passive recipient of norms and socializing forces. Deviance or the failure to perform roles adequately is treated as the result of forces which are happening to the person, and not the result of rational self–interested action or some combination. This orientation is particularly vexing when it comes to interpreting activities which are basically political. Often, the public or political realm is treated as derivative of private life, and political actions are "predicted" by attributes of the social environments in which people are situated. When this mentality is turned toward social reforms, we get evaluations which describe how ineffective treatments are and sociological discussions of the irony of how programs produce the very behaviors they were designed to extinguish. If one began with more political and rational assumptions about human behavior, rather than passive assumptions, outcomes might look quite different. If public action is spurred by self–interest, (i.e., the desire of groups to maintain themselves and gain power), then reforms might look far more like *means,* rather than *ends.* In other words, receiving a foundation or federal grant may be just as important as the goals which the grant is meant to produce. Receiving the grant may be an end, rather than a means.

If we can assume that community organizations are essentially political entities, then Wilson's approach to political organizations supplies a starting point for understanding group behavior in the reform process.

> The fundamental assumption made here is that organizations seek to maintain themselves. This objective requires, in turn, that associations be able to lay claim to a more or less stable supply of resources—members, money, issues, causes, and privileged access to governmental or other relevant institutions (Wilson, 1973, p. 262).

Community organizations seek funding not only to achieve ends (goals), but also to maintain themselves. Often the members or constituents of the organization produce these resources for maintenance. Members supply the money, leadership, and commitment that are needed. When members supply resources, they can decide whether the political direction of the organization is acceptable. Members can exit from the organization if they are dissatisfied with either the rewards they receive or the direction the group takes. Organizations attempt to retain membership through political development. If the politics of the group are diluted in the pursuit of maintenance, then membership will decline, especially if the organization offers few incentives beyond these goals. Organizations of the less well–to–do have, by definition, a more serious maintenance problem than more well–to–do organizations because their members have fewer resources of all types. This lack of resources constrains the contributions, both of time and money, that members can make to the organization.

Yet, seeking other means of sustaining such organizations imposes special problems. For example, while many organizations seek external support (grants, contracts, and large gifts), maintaining an organization through this external support may affect the group's political development. When resources for maintaining the organization come from outside, organizational maintenance and membership retention may no longer be closely linked. Maintenance becomes a function of satisfying the interests of nonmemoers supplying outside support as much as the satisfaction of members' needs. Thus community organizations are caught on the horns of a dilemma—they cannot rely solely on members for resources, so they must seek external support. But does this external funding enhance or inhibit the organization's capacity to achieve its political mission? The answer lies in how we think the political development of the community organization is affected by external support.

Studies of community groups and external funding fall into two camps. One group, which we call *incentivists,* assumes self–interested action on the part of the actors involved; the competing group, *dependency theorists,* relies on what they would call structural variables to account for the actions of individuals and groups. The impact of external funding depends on which perspective is employed. The incentivists see rational actors and the dependency theorists see systems, automated by a logic which determines outcomes.

The *dependency* theorists specifically argue that relying on external support for organizational maintenance undermines the capacity of community organizations to represent the interests of their constituents. However the *incentivists* argue that increased resources will generally be associated with higher membership retention: with increased resources, organizations are better able to attract and retain members because they have more collective and selective incentives for participation. Their focus is on the effects of the *level*, rather than the *sources*, of resources on membership retention. The dependency perspective suggests external support is to be avoided; the incentivist implies that it is to be sought.

The pursuit of resources should then account for many forms of collective behavior, including efforts to attract external funding. It should come as no surprise then that much of what community organizations do is done in order to maintain the group. Since social reform goals are often central to the mission of these groups, it should also come as no surprise that external funding is often secured in exchange for a promise to pursue a reform agenda. Piven (1974) made this point some years ago when she suggested,

> What appears as a government apparatus mired in confusion and ineptness is in fact a reflection of the political underpinnings of social welfare measures—measures spawned in the first place to maintain a political leadership, and then continuously adapted to a changing political environment. In that process of adaptation, public goals come to be regarded less as a set of first principles guiding action and more as a political resource. Goals can be formulated, broadened, diffused and multiplied to suit political needs.

From the community organization's perspective a reform effort is first and foremost about maintenance and what we see in the behavior of the group in getting involved is that "adaptive rationalism through which a political system and its members are maintained." There are of course other goals and objectives which the group and some of its members are also pursuing, and we will discuss these later. But it is important to begin with the notion that much of what passes for social reform becomes concrete at the community level with outside funding. That reform is seen by the recipients of the funding as the resources *necessary* for the maintenance of their organization. While many scholars have started with the formal goals of funded projects as the criteria against which to judge the behavior of the groups (evaluation and implementation research), we begin with the notion that the groups are seeking to maintain themselves through the funding the project brings and that the manipulation of formal goals are a means to achieving that end.

While the relationship between political development and maintenance is a pervasive organizational tension, the political mobilization of the poor during the 1960s raised important issues about the effects of funding sources on organizational direction. As attention focused on the effectiveness of poor people's organizations in representing those for whom they purported to speak, researchers became concerned with the impact of external funding on community organizations.

> ... [T]he dilemma for community organizations of the poor is that often they must trade their autonomy in action and goal creation for the capacity to initiate and maintain the organization (Lipsky and Levi, 1972, p. 176).

The reason these organizations *must* trade autonomy for maintenance has to do with the nature of community organizations and the distinctive, uniquely political mission imputed to them by dependency theorists. The distribution of wealth and power leaves few resources available to the poor; this lack of resources makes them relatively powerless to bargain for change, although without change they remain weak.

> ... community organizations form an instrument for reflecting particular interests, that there are different interests in society, and that lower–income community organizations are necessarily directed at changing the system. The determination of the effectiveness of these organizations should be measured by whether their strategies, structures, and actions are rational by these particular ends (Gittel, 1980).

Basic maintenance needs—the pervasive lack of resources and the short-term, urgent needs of organization members—curtail the extent to which low–income groups are able to challenge the system. But the adversarial nature of this mission presents a further constraint on low–income organizations: the likelihood that it is in the objective interest of the state to repress, diffuse, or deflect such demands. In the dependency view, community organizations of the poor are contending with an active state, one sensitive to threats to its legitimacy, but resistant rather than responsive to demands for changes in existing resource allocation. When the state responds to discontent and redistributive demands, the response may be cyclical to the extent that its legitimacy is threatened (e.g., Piven and Cloward, 1977), and cooptive to the degree that such demands can be channeled by granting groups selective access and representational monopolies.

From this perspective, the community organization is not an effective political resource because the need for organizational maintenance, under these conditions of structural disadvantage, undermines the organization's effectiveness in pursuing its necessary mission—to challenge the status quo. Where individual resources are low and where the struggle for power matches the weak against the strong, serious oppositional behavior is quite difficult to maintain. While ideological commitments can and do play major motivational roles in sustaining political participation and activity, they may not be enough to maintain adversarial stances over time in the face of these competing demands and powerful adversaries.

External funding only exacerbates these structural dilemmas. The dependency on external resources to meet organizational maintenance needs puts community organizations in a precarious situation since those who control the grants, gifts, and contracts on which these groups depend often have no interest in seeing their bargaining position improved. When this external support is from government sources, it may deflect groups into activities that end up legitimating the status quo rather than changing it. By implication, if resources were available from the membership, the goal displacement problem would be less severe although not altogether absent.

Thus, the major conceptual relationship of interest in the dependency approach is between money and mission, specifically the effects of external funding on the political development of organizations. The presumption is that the state's objective interests ultimately are in conflict with the objective interests of community organizations. The extent to which the level or source of money affects organizational maintenance needs is not of prime interest; membership retention gains from effective collective action rather than alleviation of the costs of membership. These arguments lead to the conclusion that externally funded community organizations cannot be a political resource for the poor because, in depending on outside support for maintenance, these groups weaken their capacity to challenge the status quo. Low–income groups are left, then, either to apathy and cynicism or to spontaneous forms of resistance. Bargaining and negotiating in the political arena are dismissed as irrelevant at best and counterproductive at worst. Conventional politics is off limits for the poor (Alford and Friedland, 1975); disruptive politics may gain some concessions (Piven and Cloward, 1980) but at great cost.

The incentivist perspective marries pluralist theories of group behavior with rational choice views of individuals' decisions to participate in political activities. Assuming rational, self–interested individuals, the incentivists pose the question: "Why do people join interest groups?" (Moe, 1980). They answer by looking to the incentives that would motivate a person to pursue his or her goals through collective action in these individual decisions; the individual's calculation of the incentives and disincentives associated with joining and maintaining an organizational membership is the theoretically interesting issue.

While there are important differences among incentivists (Moe, 1981), they share a reliance on certain concepts. First, political organizations are the sum of their members. If one is to understand those organizations and their mission, one must grasp the needs and interests of those who belong. Rather than assuming objective interests, incentivists perceive organizations as the instruments of individuals, each trying to maximize his own individual benefits. Also, incentivists assume that the individual goals of members add up to organizational goals. External resources merely increase the odds that members will achieve their personal objectives by improving the resources available relative to the demands being made.

Rich (1980), however, does link maintenance to external funding from an incentivist perspective.

> Examination of the distribution of neighborhood organizations among communities of different class standings indicates that exclusive reliance on voluntary form places lower–class communities at a disadvantage relative to middle–class groups because such organizations are less often available to overcome the negative dynamics created by a low resource/demand ratio. The availability of more powerful forms of organization and access to outside resources could short circuit this dynamic by making collective actions more predictable and thus increasing the probable effectiveness of concerted effort in altering community conditions (p. 590).

In the incentivist approach, there is no assumption that low–income groups will, or should, differ from upper income groups in organizational mission or maintenance needs, only that the support of external funding would increase their resource/demand ratio to a level making concerted action more likely and more effective. Maintenance and mission are complementary rather than antagonistic functions for incentivists.

This line of reasoning suggests that community organizations have little or nothing to lose from outside funding. Most contemporary studies of crime prevention in community organizations assume the incentivist perspective. Support from outside organizations only increases the resource/demand ratio and benefits both the organization and the community it serves.

The effects of the *source* of funding on organizations with low resource/demand ratios are not compelling issues for the incentivists. A major reason for this inattention is the pluralist notion of the state that imbues the incentivist approach. Where the dependency theorists see public funds as top–down efforts to structure demands, the incentivists see these resources as increasing the capacity of groups to garner benefits for members. The distribution of benefits allocated by public authority is interpreted as the sum of demands made on the political system rather than reflecting particular legitimacy needs of public authority. Thus, low–income organizations' effectiveness in shaping policy responses and gaining these benefits is a function of their ability to express their needs. Granting funds to such organizations is seen as increasing this capacity. In the absence of a theoretical argument about structural relations between public authority and class–based groups, incentivist arguments emphasize the programmatic successes of efforts rather than the interaction between funders and recipients and the concomitant deflection of mission objectives which often take place.

The results, with a few important exceptions, have been the production of program evaluations which focus on crime–related outcomes and the participatory patterns of those who get involved in the crime prevention activities (Yin, 1979). This incentivist temperament has dominated the debate on using community organizations for crime prevention.

Dependency theorists have taken a dim view of community organizations and externally supported crime prevention primarily because the structural interest of the state obstructs the pursuit of class–based missions. Studies in the '70s and '80s from this perspective confirmed the theoretical judgment that goals would be deflected and organizations uncoupled from the interests of poor communities they sought to serve. Thus our scholarship on crime prevention and community organizations either omitted discussion of the effects of external funding on the missions of community groups or assumed that cooptation was inevitable. The incentivist perspective shifts our debate about crime prevention and community organization towards a neutralized discussion of tactics about how to get more people involved in "obviously" beneficial efforts. The dependency perspective, on the other hand, produces an isolationist position arguing for noninvolvement, when poor communities are starved for resources and victimized routinely.

By taking a pragmatic interactionist position, we can move beyond the stale debates of the last decade. Community organizations pursue goals that dictate how they interact with outside agencies. Those goals include the maintenance of their organization, the retention of members and the improvement of their political position. Resources are sought to achieve these goals. External funders while sympathetic to some of these objectives establish programmatic objectives which are tied to the receipt of the funding. Social reform is the negotiations between funder and recipient organization, as well as community residents, local elites and intellectuals. How that reform is perceived depends in large measure on the position from which it is viewed and what the observer expected from the reform. The importance of the political dimension cannot be overemphasized. Groups that are funded are pursuing their overall advantage in terms of their political environment. It is the external funder who enters that world on the community organization's terms.

Dependency theorists dismiss the political benefits which community organizations gain and treat the groups as victims, overwhelmed by state interests and opportunistic leaders. This approach treats goals, especially formal ones, as ends, rather than means that can be changed and adapted as the political situation warrants. Perhaps this is due to an underlying functionalism which haunts much dependency theorizing, but it is this reification of goals and purposes that overlooks the give and take of politics. On the other hand, the incentivists misrepresent the political agenda of ruling elites and funders and see no objective limits to proposed reforms.

Our approach suggests that the key issues are not whether a group does or should accept external funds but whether a group is politically developed enough to pursue constituency interests that will enhance its ability to retain membership and build legitimacy. Organizations must develop the capacity to make demands that are relevant to their membership; external funding in itself cannot retain those members without such demands. Many types of groups receive external funds, but only those with sufficiently developed political strategies appear able to use those funds in ways that attract and retain members. Groups' political skills and capacities, that is, their political development, are the intervening variables determining whether external funds improving resource/demand ratios will actually lead to greater membership retention. Neither community groups nor community scholars should obsess about the morality or hazards of external funding or measure groups' purity in terms of their funding linkages; rather the attention of both would be more fruitfully directed to barriers to effective identification, articulation, and advocacy of constituent interests.

The incentivist and dependency approaches too frequently treat the politics of the organization as derivative. In doing so, they underestimate the extent to which political activity shapes the economic and psychological context of organizational behavior. Both the incentivists and dependency theorists treat politics as a dependent variable "caused" by the interests of individuals or classes.

The politics of community organizations in America are deeply affected by the relative supply of resources at their disposal. Local organizations face considerable odds when competing in the conventional political arena but it is important to remember that what limits those politics is the group's political development and how well it negotiates with others, not the award of a government or foundation grant. External funding derives its impact from the politics of the pragmatic interactions between organizations.

There are five community organizations which compose the heart of this study. These groups had been part of a coalition, spearheaded by a civic organization which applied for funding to the Ford Foundation to continue the coalition's work on what is known as "community crime prevention." All the groups which comprise our study had been involved with this coalition through over a year of funding from a federal agency, so they had some experience with crime prevention activities and the civic organization was anxious to continue the project.

The focus of the proposal the civic organization sent to the foundation was something called "Neighborhood Watch." The director of the crime prevention program for the civic group, the Citizens Information Service (CIS), felt that this activity would be the best thing for the groups to do.

> I mean my position gives me the power, especially in the absence of clear policy directions in CIS, to make lots of small decisions which add up to—I could have picked another program this far and I think I could have done it and I think somebody in this position could have. What I want to underline is that I have—you know, that it is not a subjective thing. To the best of my ability, I've tried to emphasize the program block watch which is, on the evidence, best for people in the neighborhoods.

Each community group would receive roughly $25,000 a year to implement this new activity in a new part of the "turf" of the community group. They were obliged to raise an additional 25 percent in matching funds from other sources. Ford had become interested in this area of community crime prevention and was funding several programs across the country. Negotiations between CIS and Ford were productive and relatively straightforward, with the foundation insisting on an evaluation by an outside group (the authors of this book) and CIS finding this acceptable. Each community group in the coalition had to make the decision that staying involved with the Ford grant was worth their while, that the resources obtained were worth the costs incurred in staying involved, and once that decision was made that these estimates were correct as experience increased. In doing this study we selected out the ten groups involved in the coalition which were larger and more politically developed, in order to look carefully at the interactions, both within each organization and between organizations. Each group had contracted to do a certain amount of crime prevention on which they were going to be evaluated by the authors, CIS and ultimately, the Ford Foundation. But this evaluational component was not of primary importance.

Block watch was the key ingredient for the five groups. Each placed the establishment of block watches at the top of its list of things it sought to do with the crime prevention money. Yet each defined that work in ways which fit the current activities and philosophies of the group. The accommodation between what the groups aimed at doing and how they actually did block watch was shaped by the political development of the group itself. The story of the crime prevention program is the story of this interaction between the different organizations and the ideas which were the "currency" of their interaction. Block watch was something they all said they would do, but the doing of the program was open to wide differences of interpretation and capacities to accomplish what they sought to do.

Several authors have suggested that by buying into the "victimization perspective" and the strategies it suggests, community organizations are moving away from activities which would serve the interests of the community members. Crime prevention activities that attack issues of inequality, police brutality and social injustice might be closer to the needs of the community members than block watches, security surveys and property making programs which can do little to change the number of jobs in the community, the quality of education and the amount of political power which community members possess. By deflecting the community organization towards the victimization type program, the argument can be made that such activities are deflecting the group from goals that are in the true interests of the community. Crime prevention had in the past been a way to attack the status quo, but the kinds of things for which community organizations can obtain resources are not necessarily the same as those which actually improve that community's political power. Thus, in the case of crime prevention, the maintenance needs of the group can work to deflect the groups from their important goals.

The suggestion that the reform effort introduced by CIS and the Ford Foundation was open to various outcomes as a result of factors far beyond the control of CIS and the problems of implementation (in an ironic turn) was partly created by the interactions between CIS and the community organizations. The limitations of the role CIS could play in coercing the groups to comply with its notion of what to do and how to do it were limited. Both the CIS ideology which emphasized local autonomy and leadership and the fact that the community organizations were separate organizations which depended on the Ford grant for a small part of its resources, and thus were not dependent on the Ford support for the life of the group, made control difficult.

Within each group the neighborhood watch activity had different homes. This positioning was the result of factors which were also outside the control of the funding and coordinating agencies. The personnel assigned to administer the neighborhood watch was also outside the control of these agencies and again their abilities and power within the organization to get things done varied considerably. Finally, the communities in which the neighborhood watch was introduced varied in their interest in and reactions to the watch. Depending on who came to the watch meetings and the abilities of the leaders of these meetings, people got excited about the watches or they felt little interest. This variability in attitude affected whether the watches were actually put in place. Once in place, it was then important to see if these organizational activities actually affected the behavior of those who were engaged in criminal activity. All these factors interacted to determine the effectiveness of the neighborhood watch, and most of them were beyond the control, much less the influence, of the organization charged with the overall administration of the program. Indeed, interactions at each level of activity affected the possibilities of success and failure at other levels of interaction. The goal of more cohesive and secure communities, through neighborhood watch, was "constructed" as the interactions between and within organizations evolved.

Reform then was manufactured by the community groups in terms of how the intervention, block watch, met the political needs of the leadership of the group. These leaders negotiated what they would and would not do in order to keep the resources contributed by the reform effort. In this way, the groups created the reforms as they went along interacting with CIS, each other and the members of their communities. The history of each group's political development dictated what kind of activities would be beneficial in recruiting and retaining members and how the neighborhood watch activity could be woven into the structure of the group without undermining the decisionmaking apparatus and ideology which had evolved. These constraints set the parameters for the negotiations and compromises which took place over the period of the year which encompasses our study.

In the next chapter we will describe how the coordinating agency which received the grant from the Ford Foundation related to the five community organizations charged with implementing the Neighborhood Watch.

# 3

# Coordination and Reform

The Citizens Information Service (CIS) of Illinois was the recipient of a major grant from the Ford Foundation. This nonprofit group, which was a spin-off of the League of Women Voters in 1953, had served as the catalyst for the formation and funding of the Urban Crime Prevention Program (UCPP). It also provided leadership and guidance for the groups as they went from government funding to foundation support, and it was instrumental in giving the groups both a sense of direction about what they could accomplish in the area of crime prevention, and the legitimacy to compete for external support.

A little history is useful to place the current discussion in the context of what CIS and the five groups we studied had been up to for the three years prior to analysis. In September of 1982, the CIS was awarded a substantial sum of money ($550,000) in two separate grants to act as an umbrella organization for the activities of ten community groups that had been selected by an LEAA–ACTION program for a pilot program to do crime prevention (LEAA is an acronym for Law Enforcement Assistance Administration). Over a year of work had gone into putting that proposal together and finding the groups that wished to be involved in an area relatively new to community organizations. The competition for those dollars was not only tough at the national level, but there were several other coalitions of Chicago groups that were vying for funding. That grant ended prematurely seventeen months later and CIS then set out to find more funding to keep the coalition of community groups going. The search for continuing support culminated in a concept paper that was sent to Ford in February, 1982. On the basis of that paper, the Foundation agreed to support the groups and CIS for another two years.

The Citizens Information Service requested several years of support from the Ford Foundation for ten community organizations to implement a community crime prevention program. The first award was made through an annual grant of about $200,000 to CIS with the understanding that successful completion of the first year would lead to more support ($350,000). Each group received about $25,000 a year. We studied the project during this first year of operation, observing how the groups introduced the crime prevention efforts and evaluating the impacts of the projects on the target communities. Negotiations with Ford were straightforward and cordial. CIS submitted a short "concept paper" to Ford in February, 1982 outlining what they intended to do and after a short period of negotiation, the grant was awarded. The foundation had little interest in reshaping what the groups proposed to do and accepted the concept paper as the substance of the grant proposal. The ten groups which had been working together with CIS for the previous seventeenth months under funding from the federal government agreed to participate in the Ford submission, and suggested what they wanted to accomplish under the Ford funding.

Since the concept paper only had the barest outline of what the groups were going to do and how they would relate to each other and CIS, there was much that had to be negotiated between the groups and CIS once the grant was awarded. CIS proposed a structure which extended the old organization they had used under the federal support to the new grant. This involved the establishment of a steering committee made up of the presidents or their designates of all the community groups which were participating plus some outsiders with expertise or interests which were relevant to the project (academics, police officials, etc.). This group was supposed to set the policy directions for the project, although they had no formal authority within CIS or with Ford. A parallel committee was also established which was composed of the directors of each of the crime prevention programs within each community organization. In several cases there were personnel overlaps between the membership as presidents became crime prevention directors or presidents designated the crime prevention director to be their designate to the steering committee.

The steering committee was to make policy for the project and the directors were to carry that policy out. CIS hired a local organizer to direct the entire project and he set the tone and agenda for both groups. The president of CIS, an unpaid volunteer, chaired the steering committee initially and worked closely with the paid director of UCPP. Financial control of the project remained with CIS, and the director of the crime prevention program for CIS played a major role in directing the activities of the groups.

The volunteer leadership which comprised the steering committee was to guide the project, while the directors were to implement the goals of the steering committee. This formal structure was at odds with the structure created by the awarding of the grant to CIS, for the contractual arrangements loomed very large in CIS's mind, necessitating strict rules for the dispersal of funds and the reporting of financial and substantive information. The steering committee could set policy, but only under the watchful eye of the president and crime program director. Both were quick to let the groups and their representatives know what "Ford" would think of different ideas that were discussed, and how "Ford" would react to the speed at which they were making progress towards their goals. CIS made it clear through these meetings and their interactions with the groups independently, what would be acceptable to the granting agency and to them.

The original concept paper was rather general about what the groups would do during the period of funding. It suggested that building community cohesion would reduce crime and have other beneficial effects on the neighborhood. It suggested that working with the criminal justice system and having a broad–gauged approach to crime prevention was also the way to go. The CIS director of the entire project focused attention on block watch as the approach that should be pursued.

Given his review of the field and what was known about community crime prevention, he felt strongly that block watch was the most viable approach. Block watch might have an impact on crime and it was something that all the groups could do, with the proper technical assistance from CIS. The evidence on which he based this decision was skimpy at best, with one unpublished paper (Kohfeld, Salert, and Schoenberg, 1980) playing an important role, because it claimed success for the technique.

CIS had not often been involved in providing outside monies for other organizations prior to its involvement with the crime prevention field. The group had spent most of the previous thirty years offering citizenship training to people in low–income areas. This training focused on developing leadership skills among low–income people and that was done through classes and other educational activities. Trying to coordinate the activities of community organizations to perform new and innovative programs under its auspices was new for CIS and its volunteer leadership. CIS hired Arthur Sims, a veteran Chicago organizer, to administer the government–funded program, and it was Sims who orchestrated the production of the Ford proposal with able help from the volunteer leadership of CIS. Sims took the responsibility for moving the groups toward the proposal and, more importantly, he coordinated the operations of the project in the last months of government support as well as through the period of the evaluation and beyond.

CIS and Sims saw their primary responsibility as the organizational development of each of the groups. The goal was to produce or help to produce democratically run organizations that could be counted on to represent their constituents to the powers that be at the metropolitan level.

That goal and the assumptions that underlie the commitment to it are the subject of this chapter. For it is this commitment to a middle–class notion of city reform that supplied both the positive and negative influences on the groups and how they went about their business. There are three ways that this commitment affected the activities of CIS. First, they placed great reliance on the responsible expenditure of funds and the dispersal process. CIS took its responsibility as fiscal agent very seriously and communicated that seriousness to the groups involved. Thus the keeping of books and the accounting for the dollars was a top priority for CIS. This came both from previous grant experience with the federal government and their general view of what and how groups should go about their business. Fiscal responsibility was a high priority.

Next they saw their expertise in the project as having to do with training the groups, particularly their boards, on how to carry out their business democratically. This concern followed from the long–standing interest in the teaching of citizenship skills to low–income people. CIS felt and Sims did too, that they could educate the groups about the importance of doing their business openly and fairly. This thrust involved expanding and democratizing the boards of directors of each organization and providing the groups with the sense that their effectiveness depended on the careful presentation of the projects that they were interested in.

Finally, CIS wanted to draw the groups into a commitment to the programs to which they had committed themselves in the proposal. It was one thing for the groups to agree to be a part of the proposal; it was quite another to spend the grant monies doing crime prevention. This involved getting them to take seriously the targets they had set for themselves. Much of the time the groups spent together was focused on achieving commitment to policy goals rather than implementation. Getting the groups to commit themselves to the overall objectives of the program was Sims' primary objective.

The groups were confronted with what we call a "democratic proceduralism" which pervaded all aspects of the interaction between the groups and CIS. Sims focused the discussions between the groups and CIS on building a consensus around the crime prevention goals that were outlined in the proposal to the Ford Foundation. He suggested what Ford's requirements were for the successful completion of the grant, mostly on the basis of his previous experience with government agencies, and attempted, through the procedures he introduced to meet those requirements, to shape how the organizations performed their contractual obligation. This was by no means a heavy–handed process. Representatives of each group were allowed to speak their minds and discuss their differences so long as they met their procedural obligations (accounting, reporting, attendance, etc.).

Sims was so intent on maintaining his control over what transpired and keeping his commitment to the appearance of democratic decisionmaking that a slow, cumbersome process ensued which saw much time and energy spent on gathering a disgruntled consensus that gave the appearance of cohesion rather than the actual thing. This dilemma follows not so much from a lack of CIS leadership but rather from the ideology of the group.

The CIS steering committee meetings were instructive in this regard. Formally, this group was supposed to represent the decision makers for each of the groups involved. Often, each group was represented by the person charged with the implementation of the block watch program. Sims spent much of the time at these meetings trying to persuade the groups that they ought to take the goals they had set for themselves seriously and that there was much that the project could do for them. In meeting after meeting (especially of the Project Directors), the group was attentive to the issues of how to count the number of block watches they were involved in and other exhortations about the necessity of committing to the overall block watch goals they had set for themselves. Clearly, Sims had pushed the block watch program as the central pillar of the project. He had decided that this was an approach that was "best for the people in the neighborhoods," and was acceptable to the funding agency. He then faced the problem of getting the groups to commit to the proposed objectives. This came down to producing the number of block watches they had promised. He did this by developing a chart of "watch foundings" and sending the project directors forms on which they could describe their progress. This meant that much of the steering committee's and project director's time was spent on discussions of how well the groups were doing (productivity) and whether they could count certain activities as appropriate (get credit for administrating them). Sims saw the main benefits of CIS leadership as coming down to "giving the community groups experience in managing and using resources and helping them get the resources" and in developing a coalition of community groups that could stand independently of CIS, with Sims at the helm. Sims' goals gave the shape and intention to the CIS efforts and to much of what went on with the groups. But, with the exception of one organization, these goals were never translated by the groups into serious efforts to implement the block watch in the designated areas.

Marris and Rein (1967) claim that a social reformer needs three elements to have a chance at succeeding. First, he must put together a coalition sufficient to accomplish his goals. Second, he must respect our democratic tradition which requires that each person ought to have a voice in formulating the reform as it affects him. Finally, his proposals must be rational. Sims had all the elements in place, but each unraveled in practice. Indeed the commitment to the democratic tradition led to letting each group have the autonomy to decide how much and what it wanted to do. With the exception of one group that would not allow CIS to provide them with "technical assistance," all the groups were allowed to maintain their funding. Sims and others from CIS tried to persuade the groups to go along with them, but they stopped short of dropping them if they ignored efforts to conform to the goals they had committed themselves to in the project. This insistence on the democratic imperative literally insured that little could be done if the groups did not enter the project with the skills to achieve their goals. From Sims' perspective the block watch was the minimal compliance goal he had to achieve to keep the funding agency happy with the project. But, achieving this goal was not something he actually knew how to do; however, he could achieve the CIS goals of technical assistance and the development of the independent coalition. As he came to understand that Ford was not like his previous funders in demanding compliance with formal goals, he relaxed his pressure on the groups that they achieve the level of block watches that they had promised. Even if Sims had wanted to coerce compliance he would have had difficulties, for the threat of disaffiliation could only be used once and the costs of disaffiliation could be borne by all the groups. Losing the Ford grant would have hurt all the groups but doing what they had promised would have hurt some of the groups more, for it would have drawn significant resources away from other, more important activities.

The national culture of social reform to which CIS is linked, both through its own ideology and through the Ford grant, is shaped by an abiding interest in process and technique. The way one does things outweighs the result of the process. The emphasis is on neutralizing the provincial aspects of political activity and coming up with democratic procedures for implementing programs. The need is for "cosmopolitans" who reside in urban communities, that is, people who are interested in linking directly into the world of categorical grants and generalizable principles of operation. Banfield and Wilson (1963) saw this coming over a generation ago when they discussed the way urban politics were changing, moving away from the patronage and self–interested politics of the big–city machine and towards the professionalism of middle–class culture. Planning and procedures were fast replacing the quid pro quo of earlier periods. The search for solutions to problems in a cooperative manner with the public interest guiding the effort is the hallmark of this middle–class approach. Authority is held by those who are best qualified and have the technical expertise to argue their case before public opinion. Poor communities must learn to play this game or not play at all (Banfield, 1963). While there are a few cities in which this style has not become pervasive, it certainly has dominated the method of operation between city reformers and the national reform culture. If neighborhood groups are going to become a part of this culture and reap its benefits, they must learn to play by these rules.

CIS had the obligation, as they saw it, to train the community organizations to operate within this culture, and much of what they did to the groups was to acclimate them to these values and the skills that are needed to operate in this milieu. This is the root of the most troublesome aspect of the accommodation process, for the groups and their leaders drew their political strength from the capacity to influence locals and have influence within the neighborhood power structure. Personal relationships and the connections that develop over time are the stuff of a successful community leader. Expertise is less important than the ability to act as a liaison between the people they represent and the bureaucracies that impinge on their daily lives. While the new culture can lead to important benefits, it detracts from the sources of strength that the community leadership depends upon to recruit new members and maintain the organization. Thus the middle–class culture works at cross–purposes with the needs of the leadership at key points. For example, the organizations have to pay attention to CIS. Much time was taken up not only with meetings with CIS and the evaluators, but there was considerable paperwork that was said to be important. Whether the trade–off is in the best interest of the groups is not clear, although they received substantial resources in return for the time and effort they put into the process. While the groups certainly lost time and manpower for their efforts and were often less than enthusiastic about what they got in return, they do have the money.

Perhaps the central point remains that for the groups to succeed, it was the local residents whom they needed to influence and to mobilize, and that was not helped by the skills CIS sought to transmit. If the provincial influence depends on personal relations within the community, then there must be tangible benefits to those who get involved. Building the organization and maintaining it depends on attracting people to the group and giving them something in return. That means strong personal relations that draw people into the group, and then deliver on some of the things that are important to the members. This includes access to the government agencies that impinge on the lives of the residents, but it also includes more personal activities around social and recreational concerns. Personal relations and the ability to produce desired outcomes attracts and sustains membership. Even if there is rapid turnover in the community, residents want to know their neighbors and feel a sense of security for their children. That evolves from personal relations and that takes time and effort. Being focused at this level means spending time building specific linkages between specific people in particular communities.

The middle–class reform sentiment can improve the communication between the local leader, municipal government, and foundations—the downtown perspective—but it cannot replace the connection that the local leader has to his or her constituency, and that is the key to the community organization's authority. For the local leader must be able to deliver local goods to the member if he/she is to stay involved, and that follows from a local reputation for power and respect. In this environment, cosmopolitan values are not respected, indeed, they have little standing when it comes to local affairs. For example, the public good on a given issue, *may* be in direct conflict with the interests of residents. New roads, urban development, and so on, may upset the neighborhood considerably. The issue may be more for the community to fight this change than to cooperate with it in the "public interest." From the larger communities' perspective, there are even smaller issues that the local leader can help with, given his clout in the community (e.g., stop signs, school problems, recreational issues, and tensions). These are the building blocks of local success, caring about the particular people and helping them with their personal issues that are locally based. The ability to do this follows from personal relationships with those who can help and a reputation for caring about those that one helps.

This problem can be conceived as another tension between autonomy and maintenance. Maintenance demands taking resources which shift the groups' activity. The mission gets reoriented in that process because the priorities are shifted by that activity. What we describe in some detail is how each of the groups handles this conflict. This problem strikes at the heart of the social reform agenda, for it involves the differing cultural needs of the organizations involved. While it was empirically resolved through the mutual accommodation process that the organizations were involved in, it has significant costs especially for the weaker groups, for they found themselves in the position of having to take the pressure more seriously and thus not developing the clout they need at the local level. Groups that were less politically developed cannot afford the time and effort that go into meeting CIS's requirements. The meetings, reports and requirements detracted from building local authority.

The reform temperament of CIS may have a lot to do with the problems the agency had with the black community organization. Since the CIS saw participation among minority groups as a way of improving services and bringing good government to the corrupt patronage system of the city, they saw no conflict between participation and rationality. If CIS could assist this black group to participate freely in the political process, then intelligent judgments on political issues would follow. Broadening community participation through democratic groups would lead to a more rational administration of services to the black community. What they failed to see is that the CIS ideology was not only not shared by the group in question, but that the outcome sought may not have been possible. Black organizations often see their political participation as a mechanism for the development of their own organizations and a way to make demands that would assert the interests of oppressed groups. The goal of self–government and political power did not easily fit the ideology of CIS. Auburn–Gresham wanted to mobilize its community and develop new elites who could articulate the interests of the black community. They were not comfortable with the more limited goals of CIS and what appeared to them to be the patronizing attitude of the latter group's leadership. Participation did not mean more democratic proceduralism to them. Rather it meant the assertion of black interests and demands.

As for the other four groups which we observed, we will look carefully at how the crime prevention activities were absorbed into the body of each organization. The business of crime prevention was a small part of the total agenda of each group. Each group wove the crime prevention program into the greater goals of building the membership and being a force in the local decision–making process. If crime prevention did not serve these ends, it undermined the purpose of the groups. This avowedly political perspective is reflected in how each of the groups went about that business. They have all developed ways of achieving their political goals through the collective problem–solving techniques. Indeed, as we will show further on, the interaction between the group and the intervention is a two–way street. Depending on where the group was before the intervention, they reacted in very different ways to the demands the program was putting on them. The amount and direction of the change appeared to be a function of the amount of democracy in each organization and the ideology of the group, that is, its political development. As the groups got more democratic and preservationist in orientation, the intervention seems to be taken more seriously and on its own terms.

The more change–oriented the group was, the less committed it was to the intervention. The main reason for this was that the politics of the group and its structure made the block watch too much of a distraction from other objectives. The intervention appeared to have an impact on the group when the group was driven by democratic principles and a preservationist mentality. The reasons for this have to do with the synchronization between the group's culture and the demands of the intervention and its culture. For those groups that have a culture that supports individual concerns about problems as the backbone of their agenda, the block watch program gave the group a way to solve problems around the issue of crime. When issues can emerge from members and crime is among those issues, a group will embrace the block watch strategy; when a group's agenda is determined from the top, and its culture is social change–oriented, it is less likely to find block watch an effective political tool.

What is the relationship between crime prevention or any other substantive program a group participates in and the political development of the group and the community it purports to represent? If political values are in conflict with program objectives and procedures, then the program will be abandoned or gutted. This conflict will be exacerbated when those political values are *localist* in perspective and the program objectives are cosmopolitan. Cosmopolitans and locals see problems differently and attack them along opposing lines. Clearly, the middle–class values of the cosmopolitans have won out, for they control the flow of money and the terms by which it is distributed. Without their help the locals would continue to fight for their political development with fewer resources. The irony of course is that the cosmopolitan reformers speak for progressive change and for the locals they seek to help, but it is that help which becomes so problematic for the groups as they seek to develop politically. It is this clash of values and the accommodation that follows that explains so much of what we saw and heard during the year of the evaluation. The cosmopolitans set the terms of the debate in ways that are, at a minimum, foreign to the groups and the way they see themselves and their activity. The locals have a narrow vision of what they are seeking and they must accommodate themselves to the demands of the national reformers, particularly as interpreted by CIS. The latter group truly sees itself as helping with that political development but in ways that contradict the values and strengths of the groups. CIS and the groups think about what they want to accomplish differently, accommodating to each other without giving up the primary vision each holds, but both are ultimately concerned with their own vision: each sees the reform process and the objectives of the grant in its own terms.

Did the groups develop politically with the support of the Ford Foundation? They did to the extent that they had the leadership and organizational resources to take advantage of the money available. Did the support lead to crime prevention? It did, to only a modest degree, because crime prevention would have come at too great a political cost if it had been given the priority suggested by the grant application. The organization and maintenance of a systematic block watch network would have been a massive effort. CIS tried to move the groups towards a commitment to the block watch goal but had neither the authority nor the proper strategy to force that commitment. CIS sought to improve the capacity of the groups to compete for resources at the cosmopolitan level and in doing so moved the groups in a direction that undermined the strengths of some of the groups among their local constituents by drawing attention and resources away from the neighborhood.

CIS faced a dilemma not uncommon among coordinating agencies, namely, that the organizational dependence created by the Ford funding conflicted with the member groups' desire for autonomy. Each community organization had to develop procedures for maximizing autonomy in areas of conflict while at the same time permitting united efforts where there were benefits to be acquired (Litwak and Hylton, 1962). The coordinating agencies themselves, like CIS, must keep autonomy and dependency in balance. They must keep the participating organizations aware of this interdependence and try to produce standardized units of the coordinated activity. If they fail to do these things, there will be no reason to coordinate, for the groups will return to independent states or merge into one organization.

It is important in this respect to remember that neither CIS nor the groups took *crime reduction* as its first priority. CIS sought to assist the groups in becoming more "cosmopolitan," that is, more capable of doing business with downtown interests including city hall. This meant creating a decision–making structure both in the project and in each organization that maximized rationality and democratic processes. They focused on compliance with imputed grant requirements to move the groups in that direction. The groups for their part sought the external funding to build their organizations politically. To the extent that they took the block watch seriously, it was seen as a tool for recruiting new members and drawing them into the organization.

Given CIS's ideological commitment to middle–class reform goals and the requirements of maintaining the coordination function, the interactions between the organizations made eminent sense. Both the Steering Committee meetings and project director meetings were shaped by these goals and requirements. The former group was intended by CIS to set the direction for the project and its future, and the latter was intended to guide the implementation process for the crime prevention activities. What both ended up doing was defining activities that they could be coordinated around (e.g., "the grid," newsletter, coalition, training, etc.).

We should remember in all of this that the Ford Foundation had made the grant to CIS and that CIS served as an intermediary between the groups and the donor. CIS asked the groups for several things in exchange for the funding. These included several procedural arrangements around the dispersal of the Ford funds and other reporting requirements (e.g., progress reports), attendance at the meetings mentioned above, and some commitment to the objectives the groups had outlined in the proposal to Ford. This was not a dependent relationship for the groups. Each community organization was a freestanding organization with a history, a philosophy, and other resources. Each protected its autonomy in matters where there was conflict and held the ultimate power of withdrawing if it was not satisfied with the arrangements. Ironically, it was the group (Auburn–Gresham) with the *fewest* alternative resources that withdrew. While the threat of withdrawing resources was there in the background, it cut both ways, for CIS saw itself as assisting the groups and did not want the embarrassment of having too few to coordinate.

CIS did many things to justify its role as coordinator. Meetings (Project Directors and Steering Committee) had more of a symbolic than instrumental function. Sims continued to press for the observance of the groups' interdependence (e.g., by emphasizing Ford's imputed desire for a coalition), for the recognition of their distinct contribution (e.g., training sessions, newsletters, the independent coalition), and by the standardization of activity (e.g., the grid and block watches). The groups all went along with this agenda for it limited their actual dependency (little was changed in their operation) and kept the conflict over autonomy to a minimum. Where the costs of interdependence went up, groups protected their independence even at the cost of continued support.

CIS was then caught in the same conflict that the groups themselves were caught in, namely that the ideology of the group and the organization of the project set the limits of what the agency could accomplish. It was committed to the notion that reform could be accomplished by activating the politically disenfranchised and that the groups would and could learn efficient methods of running their operation. CIS felt that it had the tools to teach and train the groups to compete in the policy arena in a more businesslike manner and that the groups would be interested in acquiring those skills. This analysis brought CIS into the crime prevention business. Once in, it was caught with few resources and methods for drawing the groups into a more systematic implementation of the program and thus were not able to produce a more concerted effort where that was necessary. If CIS demanded too much of the groups, it risked passive resistance or outright exit. CIS also believed that what was called for was getting the groups to commit to the goals of the program as laid out in the proposal. In fact, what was needed was a concerted effort to create a framework for day–to–day collaborative action, which would have allowed for a better implementation effort. Given the lack of expertise on how to organize block watches and the potential costs in pushing the groups to produce, CIS accommodated itself to a less forceful role, which involved the groups in activities but did not challenge their internal autonomy. To have done less would have meant that CIS had nothing to offer the groups but access to the money; to have done more would have violated the CIS ideological commitment to democracy and participation. Neither alternative was acceptable.

The community organizations, with the exception of one group representing a black community, found this accommodation acceptable. They gained more than they lost, trading some time and energy for support.

# 4

# The Community Organizations: The Northwest Neighborhood Federation and the Northeast Austin Organization

The next two chapters look at the community organizations that form the heart of this study. Beginning in September, 1982, these organizations received funds from the Ford Foundation to carry out community crime prevention. We present an overview of each organization, examining its history and ideological orientation, organizational structure, and major local concerns. We then look at its participation in the Ford–funded phase of the Urban Crime Prevention Program; we locate its crime prevention program within its structure, describe who got involved, and what happened. Finally, we depict how each group organized and operated its block watches. (All names used in this discussion are fictitious.)

The data for these chapters were gathered over a sixteen–month period using participant observation methods, which included interviews with community organization leaders and staff, attendance at organizational meetings such as board meetings, block watch meetings, and other crime program meetings, observation of UCPP Steering Committee and Project Director meetings, interviews with CIS staff, and review of the monthly block watch "grid sheets" which CIS required from the groups. This data is supplemented by a panel telephone survey of residents in the areas targeted for block watches and a citywide comparison group.

These chapters focus on the five groups we judged the most capable and the most inclined to carry out a block watch program, out of the original ten organizations which received crime prevention funds from the Ford Foundation at this time. These groups all had extensive experience with crime prevention and CIS under the LEAA–ACTION grant which preceded the Ford monies. Our purpose here is to illuminate the issues that were of concern to these groups and to describe how they handled the problems of urban crime and community crime prevention within the logic and structure of their organizations. We discuss the groups in descending order of ability and willingness to implement a block watch program in their neighborhoods.

## The Northwest Neighborhood Federation

Of the five groups we studied, the Northwest Neighborhood Federation (NNF) had the greatest affinity for a block watch program and its efforts to implement the program were the strongest. Located on Chicago's northwest side, the Federation was founded in 1978. A federation of six community groups, it includes the Hanson–Riis Park Neighborhood Organization, West Cragin Neighbors, Cragin Community Association, Avondale Community Team, North Avondale Organization and the Belmont–Irving Real Estate Committee. The organization's boundaries are Irving Park on the north, Armitage on the south, the Kennedy Expressway on the east and Narragansett on the west. It is an area of modest, well–kept homes on clean, tree–lined streets.

The area's population is predominantly white. Community residents are approximately 96 percent white and 4 percent black and other non–white individuals. The area targeted for the block watch program had these characteristics as well. There is an increasing representation of Hispanic residents in the southern and eastern sections of the community, which ranges from 15 percent to 25 percent of the population. Over half of the homes in the area are owner–occupied and only 4 percent had family incomes below the poverty level. Similarly, only 6 percent of area residents were unemployed and 15 percent of families were headed by females. Less than 25 percent of the residents were below twenty years of age (Local Community Fact Book, 1984).

The roots of the Federation can be traced to the formation of a citywide coalition to stop the construction of the Crosstown Expressway in Chicago in the early 1970s. The Citizens Action Program (CAP) grew out of an organization called Citizens Against Pollution, begun by Saul Alinsky's Industrial Areas Foundation (IAF). IAF was then just beginning its first organizing efforts among the white middle–class, in contrast to its earlier efforts among the poor and minorities. CAP successfully organized residents on the northwest and southwest sides of Chicago in opposition to Mayor Richard J. Daley's plans for the expressway. Residents believed their neighborhoods would be destroyed and that thousands of jobs and homes would be lost. CAP followed this anti–expressway effort with a successful "redlining" campaign which caught the imagination of other community organizations nationwide.

The experience with CAP deeply affected many residents on Chicago's

**FIGURE 4.1**

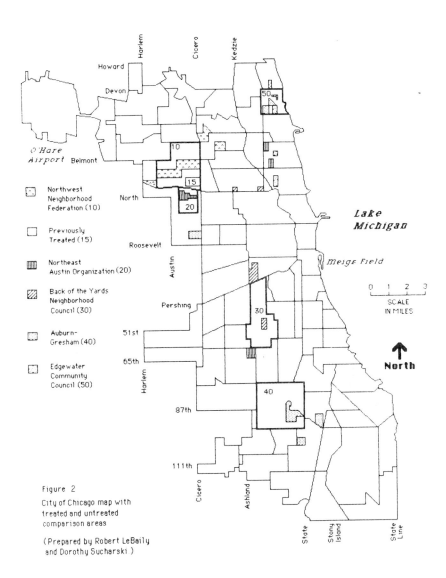

Northwest
Neighborhood
Federation (10)

Previously
Treated (15)

Northeast
Austin Organization (20)

Back of the Yards
Neighborhood
Council (30)

Auburn-
Gresham (40)

Edgewater
Community
Council (50)

Lake
Michigan

Meigs Field

0    1    2    3
SCALE
IN MILES

North

Figure 2

City of Chicago map with
treated and untreated
comparison areas

(Prepared by Robert LeBaily
and Dorothy Sucharski)

**TABLE 4.1**
**Community Areas***

| | % Black Population | | % Below Poverty Line | | No. Years Education | | Female-Headed Households | | % White Collar | | Unemployment Rate | | % Under 20 Years of Age | |
|---|---|---|---|---|---|---|---|---|---|---|---|---|---|---|
| | '70 | '80 | '70 | '80 | '70 | '80 | '70 | '80 | '70 | '80 | '70 | '80 | '70 | '80 |
| Auburn-Gresham | 69 | 98 | 8 | 13 | 12.0 | 12.3 | 17 | 36 | 18 | 48 | 5 | 13 | 41 | 39 |
| Belmont Cragin (NNF) | 0 | .1 | 5 | 4 | 10.3 | 11.9 | 12 | 16 | 19 | 48 | 3 | 6 | 28 | 25 |
| Edgewater | 1 | 11 | 6 | 11 | 12.4 | 12.8 | 13 | 26 | 40 | 65 | 3 | 7 | 18 | 21 |
| Austin (NAO) | 33 | 74 | 8 | 22 | 11.2 | 12.1 | 16 | 43 | 20 | 43 | 4 | 14 | 24 | 41 |
| New City (Back of the Yards) | 3.5 | 22 | 100 | 22 | 9.2 | 9.9 | 16 | 29 | 13 | 34 | 5 | 12 | 39 | 43 |

*Data Compiled from *Local Community Fact Book*, Chicago Review Press, 1984.

northwest side. In the summer of 1975, a group of northwest–side residents formed the Organizing Committee for the Northwest Side with the intention of founding a new local community organization. There were both positive and negative lessons from the CAP experience. On the positive side was the solid victory of ordinary citizens organized to prevent the construction of an expressway that had powerful city and state interests behind it. On the negative side was the perception that CAP was only interested in "larger" issues and was not willing to invest staff time in issues of concern to local residents. Through their involvement with CAP, residents on the northwest side met and worked with members of the Southwest Parish and Neighborhood Federation (SWPNF), a federation of eight affiliate neighborhood and parish organizations on Chicago's southwest side, founded in 1971. It was in the Southwest Parish and Neighborhood Federation that the Organizing Committee members found a model for the type of community organization they wanted to create on the northwest side.

Organizing Committee members felt there was much to learn from the SWPNF because of the decline of local organizations at that time. One of the founding organizers of the SWPNF was critical of the type of issue organizing that CAP was engaged in and believed instead that "you have to network into the fabric of the community." The members of the Organizing Committee also felt that CAP did not appreciate the local neighborhoods and the actual hope, fear, frustrations, and concerns of residents. The Organizing Committee hoped to "give voice" to those concerns through their new organization.

The members of the Organizing Committee hired an organizer from the Southwest Parish and Neighborhood Federation to begin working on the northwest side in July, 1976. He was joined by a second SWPNF organizer in January, 1977. They saw their first task as one of going around the neighborhood, interviewing residents, finding out what their concerns were, and finding out who they thought their "natural allies" were. On the basis of these interviews, plans were made to create six local neighborhood organizations.

According to one of its founders, the goal of the Organizing Committee was "to create a majority–based coalition of community organizations on the northwest side to work on a variety of issues of local concern." The organizers, however, sought to put together the local organizations first; organizing would not be around issues. As one of the "Ten Principles of Local Organizing" to which the Southwest Parish and Neighborhood Federation and the Northwest Neighborhood Federation (NNF) subscribe stated, "Issues must demonstrate the support of a majority of local residents and must be seen as parts of a whole process of organization–building, not as ends in themselves." The Northwest Federation was based on the principle of unanimity and equal participation of the six local neighborhood groups in decisionmaking. Each affiliate was free, however, to take whatever stands it wanted on local issues.

One of the founding organizers of the NNF explained why their approach to organizing was different than the more traditional Alinsky approach many of them had grown up on. "If organizing is simply to get results by having legislation changed . . . those things are important . . . but there's something more . . . it's an involvement of people . . . an inner change . . . they develop confidence and a sense of their worth." He went on to say, "democracy is with the people. If they don't feel they have ownership, our democracy is in sad shape. It's terrible when people develop an inner quality which says, 'There's nothing we can do.'"

A founding member of the Organizing Committee noted she had to be "deprogrammed" after her experience with the Industrial Areas Foundation. She said that CAP was happy with 5 percent of a community being organized. One of the satisfactions she found working with the Federation was knowing that "people have the ability to maintain the dignity and integrity of their neighborhood and know that if something came up, they will have the ability to address it." Another principle upon which the Federation was based is that "a community organization builds upon and strengthens those attributes, values, and hopes that make the people of a specific community unique." The chair of the Organizing Committee expressed this idea when she said, "White Polish residents have the right to their community. We respect and will work toward the preservation of the Hispanic community if they want that integrity preserved."

The Organizing Committee has essentially served as the fundraising group for the Federation. They hired the original staff and bought the necessary equipment. They raised money through a variety of means, including a cocktail party, a dance, and a rummage sale. At the time of our study, the Organizing Committee had six members and its chair sat on the Federation's Board of Directors. The Federation still received money from the Organizing Committee, although there was a move then toward greater direct fundraising by the Federation. In conjunction with the Southwest Parish and Neighborhood Federation, the Organizing Committee was also involved in a new neighborhood organizing effort, outside the northwest-side area.

At the start of the Ford funding, the Federation had ten full-time staff members and one part-time staff member. The overall budget of the organization was $181,000, which did not include funds received from the Organizing Committee. The Federation continued to supply staff to the local affiliates. A Federation staff member was generally responsible for one community area. Federation principles state that, "Leadership and staff must view each other as *partners* with different roles but similar goals of service on behalf of their communities." The role of staff was to "respect the communities they work for, provide technical skills for organization building, and be an essential resource for all the people of the communities they serve." The role of leaders was to "be committed to and appreciate the necessity of involving and instilling confidence in local residents to participate in the affairs of the organization." The Federation staff was headed by two co-directors who were accountable to the Board of Directors.

Each local affiliate had an elected Coordinating Council which elected four representatives to sit on the twenty-member Federation Board of Directors. The Board met once a month. The local affiliates also formed issue committees. There were federation-wide committees, as well. Everyone who lived in the neighborhoods covered by the Federation was considered a member. There were no dues. The Federation developed an extensive mailing list which reached 25,000 households. The Federation leadership saw this as a form of accountability and a means of building consensus.

The Federation was concerned with a variety of issues over the years. There were always new local issues which arose as they became a concern to residents. As one Federation leader said, "One person equals a problem, but several people equal an issue." These issues could be about a needed stop sign, an abandoned building serving as a gang hangout, an unsightly or dangerous dump site, or an apartment building with code violations. All of these had become focal points for organizing residents in an area. There were also a number of ongoing issues with which the Federation was involved. These included the issue of mortgage redlining, unscrupulous real estate practices, such as solicitation and the illegal use of For Sale signs, and what the Federation saw as the "clustered" and inequitable distribution of public low-income housing sites throughout all sections of the city. In all these instances, the Federation was largely concerned with "preserving" the quality of local life and services that the neighborhood presently enjoyed.

When we asked residents in the area targeted for the block watch (at Time 1 before the program actually began) whether "you really feel a part of your neighborhood or do you think of it more as just a place to live?", 60.5 percent said they felt part of the neighborhood. This was comparable to 61.1 percent of the citywide Chicago sample which also felt part of their neighborhoods. When we asked residents, "All things considered, what do you think your neighborhood will be like two years from now? Will it be a better place to live, will it have gotten worse or will it be about the same as it is now?", 76.2 percent said it would be about the same. This compares to 59.5 percent of the citywide sample that responded in the same way. This was clearly a stable area that its residents felt positive about.

When the Federation began, it did not focus on crime per se because "you don't organize around issues that aren't winnable." Organizers did hear complaints about crime and fears expressed from local residents that "their neighborhood was changing." At that point, the Federation simply responded to "hot spots" and put pressure on police for stepped-up activity in such areas. From the organizers' point of view, the traditional analysis about crime pointed to the underlying social and economic causes of such activity, which left few practical solutions to the problem. It was the Illinois Public Action Council that first brought the idea of a block watch program to the attention of Federation organizers. The block watch would allow them to do something not about the causes of crime but about its *effects* by reducing "opportunities" for victimization. It would allow organizers to bring the people on a block together to see what *they* could do about the problem. At the same time, block watch could provide organizers with means of recruiting more active members, working on other issues and building the organization. The Federation therefore applied for and got community crime prevention funds under the original LEAA-ACTION grant to CIS in 1981. During 1981–82, they organized sixty-seven block watches in the area south of Fullerton, an area experiencing the most "residential transition," where organizers heard complaints about rising crime rates and where they hoped bringing people together might help to confront fears about change and the unknown.

In August of 1982, the Federation was one of the ten groups brought together by the Citizens Information Service of Chicago that received community crime prevention funding from the Ford Foundation. For 1982–83, the Federation established four objectives for its crime program. The first was organizing 156 new block watches in a 209-block area with its Ford funding, as well as organizing an additional seventy-seven block watches with funds raised independently by the Federation. The 156 watches were targeted for the Cragin, West Cragin, and Hanson-Riis Park communities. When residents in these communities were asked, before the block watch program began, how they would describe the crime rate in their neighborhood, 38.6 percent said it was about average, compared with 39 percent of the Chicago citywide sample at Time 1. Fewer northwest-side residents (5.2 percent) thought it was higher than average than the citywide sample of respondents (12.3 percent).

The second objective was servicing the existing sixty-seven block watches in the Cragin, West Cragin, and Hanson-Riis Park communities. The third objective was to involve representatives from the new and existing block watches in neighborhood Anti-Crime Committees that would address local crime problems and review local police crime statistics. The fourth objective was to involve representatives from each of the local Anti-Crime Committees in a Federation Anti-Crime Committee, which could among other things, negotiate for greater responsiveness to local crime problems from the Chicago Police Department and work with other community groups involved in crime prevention efforts.

The director of the Federation's crime program was a young woman named Jennifer Miller. Having worked with another community organization after graduating from college, she was drawn to the Federation because of its approach to organizing. She was responsible for overall coordination of the crime program, as well as general organizing duties for one local affiliate. She was assisted by five other organizers who were each responsible for one local affiliate area. By July 1983, eighty–three block watches had been formed in the 209–block target area. In addition, a variety of other activities had taken place in the Federation crime program. Block watch monitoring sheets (for keeping a record of local crime activities) were sent to all block watch participants, while crime prevention bulletins were sent to particular blocks where patterns of suspicious activity had been discerned. Block watch participants worked on a number of local problems of concern to them. On one block, residents succeeded in getting an owner to fix up a run–down building, while on another, an abandoned building that had become a gang hangout was cleaned up with the help of the police. Residents on another block helped foil an attempted burglary by calling the police and other neighbors after they saw suspicious activities. In another neighborhood, residents signed petitions to force the owners of two local banquet halls to clean up their accumulating garbage dump.

Three local Anti–Crime Committees, in Cragin, West Cragin, and Hanson–Riis Park, were active throughout the year. Part of their work involved reviewing local crime statistics and looking for persistent patterns of crime. The Hanson–Riis Park Anti–Crime Committee established a special task force to collect petitions to see that an abandoned and hazardous factory would be removed. The Committee eventually monitored the demolition of that factory. The Cragin Community Association's Anti–Crime Committee conducted a survey of local residents asking about suspected drug dealing and gang hangouts. The information was turned over to the police, and, on the basis of it, twenty–three arrests were made. Members of the Federation Anti–Crime Committee each day collected block–by–block statistics for all index crimes from the local police district and then distributed the data to the local Anti–Crime Committees. As a result of a meeting with the acting police commissioner in July 1983, the Federation began receiving block by block statistics for all crimes (index and non–index) on a daily basis. At a Federation community forum on the northwest side in June 1983, newly elected Mayor Harold Washington pledged that it would now be city policy to release block–by–block crime statistics to *all* community groups in Chicago.

In August 1983, the Federation set new objectives for its second year of funding. These included forming 109 new block watches in four community areas, distributing current crime statistics to the blocks served by the program, involving residents from new and existing block watches in eight neighborhood Anti–Crime Committees, involving representatives from the local Anti–Crime Committees in the Federation Anti–Crime Committee, and participating in coalition efforts with other Chicago community groups involved with crime prevention.

By March 1984, twenty–three new block watches had been established by the Federation. Current crime statistics were mailed to approximately 2600 block watch participants each quarter. Seven local Anti–Crime Committees held regular meetings throughout the period. The West Cragin Neighbors Anti–Crime Committee was successful in getting the owner of a local banquet hall to remove accumulating trash and change the ventilation system, which was sending out black, noxious smoke into the neighborhood. Block watch participants in Avondale supported a neighbor who made a complaint against some rowdy youngsters who had been harassing area residents and accompanied him to court when he testified. In Kelvyn–Kenwell, block watch participants monitored the progress of a deteriorating apartment building and brought the case into housing court. Representatives of the Federation Anti–Crime Committee met with Chicago's new Police Superintendent to discuss police deployment policy. He promised they would receive a copy of his new deployment study and have the opportunity to give him input before any changes were undertaken.

The block watch was at the center of the Federation's crime prevention program. The watch strategy was compatible with the Federation's philosophy and approach to other issues. It allowed organizers to get down to the block level, to be responsive to residents' concerns, and to encourage them to become active in the solution to their own problems. The director of the NNF crime program noted that block watch allowed "neighbors to share the responsibility for crime." At the same time, block watch helped to build the organization by bringing in new recruits and building concern for other neighborhood issues. The Federation's crime program director concluded, "the whole program is a real plus for the organization. It brings out different kinds of people. Those who are active in the neighborhood would become involved in the NNF whether there was block watch or not, but block watch taps into those who are less active but also have concerns."

Organizers felt that it generally took two meetings to establish a block watch. The organizer responsible for an area would canvass a block, talk to residents, and find someone who was willing to host the first meeting in their home. Then flyers would be distributed door–to–door telling other block residents about the meeting and where and when it would take place.

At the first meeting, people were given a chance to meet each other, express what they saw as block problems, and then find out about the program. A second meeting would be held to solidify the watch and let new participants attend. A block watch map would be established with the names, addresses, and phone numbers of all participants. A block rep would also be chosen to attend the local Anti-Crime meetings. Block watch participants received monitoring sheets and current crime statistics on a regular basis from the Federation.

At the block watch meetings, it was often a surprise to residents to realize that they did not know many of their neighbors, even though they may have lived on the block for a long time. The watch provided them with a means to meet their neighbors and to discuss their concerns, some of which they would then realize were shared concerns. The Federation organizer helped to provide them with a new way to view the crime problem. This meant first placing crime in some factual perspective, oftentimes confirming people's worst fears. At the same time, the organizer provided a strategy to deal with the problem and gave examples of how the watch had worked effectively elsewhere to deter crime. By the end of the first meeting, participants began to see the crime problem in a new light. At the second meeting, the atmosphere generally become more friendly and social. People felt freer to talk and to interact with each other. A type of "group consciousness" emerged. From an individual problem, a "local issue" had been born. The block meeting allowed residents to perceive their troubles differently, while giving them hope that together they could do something about it. As one participant said, "It makes me feel better that something is being done." Another added, "Well, I know I'll be more careful to watch the houses of the people who are here tonight." Another concluded, "We don't see each other in winter so we need something like this."

At the local Anti-Crime meetings, the application of the block watch and the development of strategies to deal with specific problems became more explicit. At one such meeting, after a discussion of slow police response time, the woman chairing the meeting noted, "Last year we picketed at the police station to get more protection. The only people going to protect us is *us* in conjunction with the police." Then she went on to say, "The more times you call in and report a crime to the police, then it's reported as an incident on the police records. Before we got the new police commander, the response time was worse. Neighbors didn't complain. Nobody got involved, including me. I was looking for a house in the suburbs. Then I said, 'Why should I be run out of my own neighborhood?' That's when I decided block watch was the thing to do." After some discussion about an increase in burglaries in the area and whether they should send out a crime prevention bulletin alerting residents to it, the chair said, "Do you want to send out the crime bulletin? Just take them to the doors on your block. Don't hesitate to call the office if there's a problem with the police or we'll have people with guns in their homes, which is more dangerous to our children than criminals. It's one or the other. We've got to work with the police."

The most active block watch participants were recruited onto the Federation Anti–Crime Committee. Here the discussions often focused on strategies for dealing with institutional entities, such as the Chicago Police Department and insurance companies. The level of discussion and political sophistication at these meetings were quite high. At one meeting, there was a long discussion about how they could get insurance companies to lower rates to homes in areas where there was a block watch program. One participant suggested that they find out how the insurance companies compute their rates—did they use police crime statistics or the number of claims in an area? Another added that he thought "all the insurance companies were just one company anyway—one person sits at the top of the pyramid." A woman suggested that they get the Allstate representative to come out and talk to them. Another participant added, "Then lock the doors!" The organizer pointed out that if a rep came out to them, he probably would not have the authority to negotiate with them. The man chairing the meeting then suggested that they bring a group of people down to the insurance company offices—"First we could come in a group, later we could bring the pickets!" People laughed at this suggestion, but their strategy brainstorming session continued with great earnestness for some time after.

The Federation appeared to have both the motivation and the capacity to carry out its crime program. The program was competently run. The program's director kept good records detailing where watches had been formed, produced block watch maps and other supporting documentation where needed, and compiled useful quarterly reports. The crime program was integrated with other Federation activities. Organizers were responsible for a whole affiliate area, and the crime program was one of their ongoing emphases. The Federation was good at organizing blocks and seeing that follow–up and linkage occurred. The co–director of the Federation during 1982–83 believed that the watches would have to become more formalized in some manner in order for them to be maintained. The crime project director, although also concerned about maintenance, had her doubts about the block watch serving as a vehicle for other issues.

When an outbreak of gang activity alarmed residents in the south end of the Federation area in late 1983, a decision was made to go back to the original sixty–seven watches and get them more active again. Some thought was also given to the idea of a WHISTLESTOP program and senior escort service to augment existing watches.

The watch program involved many volunteers on different levels. Thousands of people attended block meetings, while more active participants became involved in the local and Federation–wide Anti–Crime Committees. In addition, the Federation supplied a good share of the volunteers to serve on the various CIS committees, including the Steering Committee, Futures Committee, and Newsletter Committee. In addition, one of the Federation's co–directors during 1982–83 served as a consultant to the other groups in the program on how to form block watches.

Of course, the Federation failed to achieve all of its own stated goals. Some of this was due to overly high expectations at the start of the program, as well as some practical organizing problems such as organizing in areas where the Federation had not been before or in areas where the residents only spoke Polish. Another factor too was the large staff turnover the Federation experienced in the summer and fall of 1983. By the end of 1983, six staff members had left and three new ones had been hired. Part of the reason for the staff turnover can be attributed to burnout and the young age of the organizers who tend to move on to other things after some experience in the "field." But the burnout was augmented by the political stress which the Federation experienced during and after the mayoral election in April, 1983. Many residents on Chicago's white, ethnic northwest side were incensed when Harold Washington failed to show up for a scheduled community forum on the northwest side a week before the election. At the time, the local and national media carried pictures of Washington being booed on the northwest side as he and Walter Mondale entered St. Pascal's church. Many of the young and often liberal organizers felt trapped between their own political sympathies for the first black mayor of Chicago and their need to remain responsive to the concerns and anxieties of northwest–side residents.

In addition, the Federation's two co–directors left during this period to take a more active role in the Chicago Neighborhood Organizing Project, which in conjunction with the Southwest Parish and Neighborhood Federation, was seeking to organize a new neighborhood area. The crime project director then became one of the Federation's new co–directors. She remained in charge of the crime program, however, and because of the staff decrease, she was also responsible for two affiliate areas. There were therefore several staff and organizational issues that affected the Federation's performance during this period. Nonetheless, the crime project was implemented in good faith. It articulated well with other Federation goals, and it produced tangible programmatic and political results. The extent to which the program had an impact on actual crime rates and how local residents felt about their neighborhood one year after the program began is discussed more fully in chapter 6. There is no doubt, however, that given the Federation's democratic structure, and its emphasis on giving "voice" to resident concerns, the block watch program was an excellent tool for them to both recruit new members and develop politically. In this case, at least, the costs of compliance with program goals were not high.

## The Northeast Austin Organization

In contrast to the Northwest Neighborhood Federation, the Northeast Austin Organization (NAO) had only moderate success with implementing a block watch program. NAO was founded in 1971 and formally incorporated in 1974. It serves an area on Chicago's northwest–central side, south of the area served by the Northwest Neighborhood Federation. Its boundaries are the Milwaukee Railroad on the north, Division Street on the south, the Beltline Railroad on the east, and Central Avenue on the west. Area residents are approximately 45 percent white, 35 percent black, and 20 percent other non–white individuals. About 22 percent of area residents identify themselves as of Hispanic origin.

The community has undergone a major racial transformation over the last decade. In 1970, area residents were almost entirely white; now over half the residents are minority group members. Thirteen percent of the current residents live below the poverty line and 9 percent are unemployed. Female–headed households represent 27 percent of the families in the area, while about 38 percent of the residents are under the age of twenty. About 46 percent of the homes in the area are owner–occupied dwellings (Local Community Fact Book, 1984).

Through the 1960s, the Organization for a Better Austin (OBA) represented most community service agencies, churches and civic groups operating within Austin. OBA was founded by Tom Gaudette, a student of Saul Alinsky. Gaudette worked with the Chicago Midwest America Institute and eventually brought community organizer Shel Trapp out to OBA. At its height, OBA was considered by many to be a model community organization. Turnout at monthly meetings would be in the range of 700 to 800 people which included area leaders, Board members, and organization representatives. The Northeast Austin Organization decided to leave OBA when it became too oriented to "black" issues in the early 1970s.

In 1971, several of the groups which broke away from the OBA formed the North Austin Community Convention. These included the Northwest Austin Organization, the Mid–Austin Council and the Northeast Austin Organization. NAO began receiving funds from Catholic Charities in 1971.

According to the current executive director of NAO, there were a lot of organizers in Chicago at the time and Catholic Charities wanted to stabilize parishes in certain neighborhoods. The Chicago Midwest America Institute was the training arm for Catholic Charities. Catholic Charities supplied the money and the organizers if a parish agreed to share half the costs.

Midge Abate was the executive director of NAO at the time of our study. She has been with the organization since its founding in 1971 and has served as its president. She took on the job of executive director in 1977. Midge served on the Citizens Action Program (CAP) Board and took classes at the Industrial Areas Foundation. She also received training from Chicago Midwest America Institute, as well as the National Training and Information Center (NTIC). She has been a long–time resident of the area.

At its founding, NAO served a community that was almost entirely white ethnic. The original goals of the organization were to "unify people" in the area and "to train people to govern themselves and work on issues that affect them." The things that concerned people were why they couldn't get mortgages for their homes, why the streets weren't repaired, and why services were so poor. NAO began organizing around issues related to local savings and loans associations, real estate practices, and services not coming into the area. Midge Abate pointed out that people had grown up in the Civil Rights Movement and the Peace Movement and had learned to question things and to speak out against injustice. She noted, "People get to appreciate their country, but they also get to question."

In the late 1970s, Northeast Austin became a "community in transition" as more minority group members began moving in and whites began to leave the area. It was then that the goal of NAO became more explicitly to stabilize the area. An NAO pamphlet stated that "our main goal has always been to stabilize and maintain a viable urban community, even though that community is economically, ethnically, and racially changing. NAO has unified the community to work on those problems that have gone unchecked and have caused the decline in our neighboring west–side communities: private and public disinvestment of resources, illegal racial discrimination, poor public education, deterioration of housing, and increase of crime."

Everyone who lived, worked, or worshipped in the area was considered a member of NAO; there were no dues. NAO had a thirty–two–member board of directors, which consisted of area leaders, officers, and committee chairs. The Northeast Austin area was divided into twelve subareas which each elected two leaders to the NAO Board. Elections were held every year. In general, there was little competition for these seats. A Nomination Committee certified the candidates, and at the annual meeting in April, the new board was sworn in. The annual meeting also provided an occasion for the president of NAO to deliver a report on the past year's activities, for an invited speaker to address the organization, and for the members to socialize. Attendance at these meetings ranged from 200 to 500 participants. At the May board meeting following the annual meeting, policy directions for the following year were set.

Individuals, block clubs, and other civic and church groups made up NAO's membership. Midge Abate pointed out that when the organization began, there really wasn't a need for block clubs because people had lived in the area a long time and knew each other. When the transition began south of North Avenue, however, NAO began organizing block clubs. Midge noted, "Block clubs add a dimension of sociability. You get to know who your neighbors are." She also added, "Integration is one thing, but resegregation is another." Area–wide community meetings were also held to deal with other problems and to provide a forum for public officials and others to account to area residents.

At the time of our study, NAO had three full–time and one part–time staff members, in addition to two part–time CETA workers. Members also volunteered their time to the organization. The overall budget of the organization during the first year of Ford funding was $45,000. Of this, $28,000 was from the Ford grant. The rest of NAO's money was raised through fundraisers such as rummage sales and bingo.

NAO worked on a variety of issues. These included security, unemployment and jobs, housing—particularly as it related to panic peddling, racial steering and absentee landlords—city improvements, the Community Reinvestment Act (an offshoot of the anti–redlining campaign), insurance redlining, victim/witness advocacy, and voter registration. Security and crime, especially as it involved youth in the area, was a top concern of the organization.

According to Midge Abate, "Crime has always been an issue here." She believed that security was the key issue for most people. As she noted, "The fear of crime will move people faster than anything else." It was for this reason that block clubs were begun in the southern half of NAO's area. Midge emphasized that "you're safe nowhere unless you make it safe for yourself." Midge considered the area south of North Avenue to be stabilized and integrated with a white population that ranged from 30 percent to 40 percent. NAO then began concentrating its efforts on establishing block clubs north of North Avenue.

NAO did a variety of things related to crime and security. It had a Citizen's Patrol which operated on weekends and involved two people each in three cars. They drove around the neighborhood and reported any suspicious activity to a bay station in the NAO office. NAO also made use of the "Area Alert" signs they originated five years before. They were also involved through their block clubs with painting addresses on the backs of garages so the police could locate houses more easily. A number of activities were directed specifically at the youth in the area, as well. These included a Youth Club, a Rent–A–Kid jobs program, and counseling sessions for first offenders which the police conducted in the NAO office. NAO also held community–wide workshops on such topics as burglary, gags, drugs, and self–defense.

NAO was also concerned with police reform. Midge pointed out that there needed to be the right type of police out on the streets, police who were physically and psychologically fit. She saw NAO acting as a monitor on the police. NAO did some of the work of the police—that is "they served as their eyes and ears"—but they could not replace the police. Midge therefore saw community crime prevention as a significant factor in the reduction of crime, especially as financial problems caused cutbacks in police services in urban areas. Midge sat on the 25th Police District Steering Committee in Chicago, the State's Attorney's Advisory Board, and the Chicago Crime Commission.

NAO received funding under the original LEAA–ACTION grant to do community crime prevention in its area; they used this money to organize sixty–seven out of one hundred six neighborhood blocks into block clubs and to pursue other crime prevention activities. NAO was also part of the ten organizations that, under the CIS umbrella, received funding from the Ford Foundation to continue their community crime prevention efforts. Under the Ford funding, NAO set the goal of organizing the remaining thirty–nine blocks in its area into block clubs which would use the block watch, as well as continuing its other crime prevention programs.

Midge Abate was director of the crime program for NAO, as well as executive director of the organization. Besides Midge, there was a full–time VISTA worker and a part–time NAO staff member who worked on crime. There were also volunteers who got involved at the block level, with the CB patrol, and with the youth program. Both Midge and the VISTA worker were involved with organizing and maintaining block clubs. Plans were being formulated for area leaders to assume a bigger role in maintaining block clubs also.

From January 1983 through February 1984, NAO organized twenty–three blocks into eight block clubs with block watches. According to our survey, 69 percent of the residents in the target area were white, 8 percent were black and other non–white individuals, and 23 percent were Hispanic. Midge told us that early on, people north of North Avenue were not particularly interested in forming watches, as the neighborhood seemed relatively untouched by the transition that occurred south of North Avenue. (By 1980, almost 75 percent of the residents south of North Avenue were minority group members.) Not long after, however, the transition did begin to affect blocks north of North Avenue. Midge observed that the fear of transition had resulted in panic, as real estate agents tried to scare people into selling their homes with images of falling property values. Other neighborhood residents still looked to the block clubs as a way to stabilize the area and to gain some control over the neighborhood. Even then, Midge pointed out the difficulty of organizing the area as people were preparing to move out. During the summer of 1983, NAO held "open air meetings" on street corners because people were fearful of meeting in "strangers'" homes. While some of the newer residents came out of city housing projects and had other bad experiences which made them afraid to meet with their neighbors, many of the older residents were equally fearful of meeting with their new neighbors in their homes.

This instability and fear was reflected in our survey results at Time 1. When we asked residents in the area targeted for the block watch program whether you "feel a part of your neighborhood or do you think of it more as just a place to live?", 43 percent said they felt a part of the neighborhood, compared to 61 percent of the Chicago city sample as a whole. When we asked what they thought the neighborhood would look like two years from now, 51 percent said they thought it would be worse, compared to 15 percent of the Chicago city sample. When we asked about the amount of crime in the neighborhood over the past year, 41 percent said it had increased, compared to 17 percent of the Chicago city sample.

Creating dialogue and cooperation between neighbors was at the heart of NAO's strategy on block clubs, and block clubs formed the essential component of their approach to crime problems in the area. NAO's orientation to crime indicated a concern with "preserving" the quality of neighborhood life, even within an environment that was changing racially and economically. At the same time, NAO also had concerns about social change issues, such as rising unemployment, illegal racial discrimination, and public and private disinvestment of resources in local communities. Its emphasis, though, on local participation and its focus on local issues allowed crime to emerge as a major issue for the organization, an issue that was taken up by both the white and black members of the organization.

For example, a young black man who was a NAO Board member brought up a problem he felt was going unattended at one monthly Board meeting. The man, wearing a Harold Washington–for–Mayor button, said that his business necessitated his driving around a lot at night and there were certain street corners where there were always groups of kids hanging out, sitting in cars, drinking beer, blasting radios. He wanted to know why the police weren't doing anything about this. He himself had seen squad cars go by and not even stop. He said, "It doesn't look like the policemen are doing their jobs to me." Another Board member added that they needed more cooperation from the police. A third noted that when they told the police they have a problem in the area, the police said there were no gangs in the area. Midge urged people to volunteer for the CB patrol.

At a block meeting held in the home of long–time white residents of Northeast Austin, another young black man served as the chair. He opened the meeting by saying that it was important for everyone to participate on their blocks and in this club. He said, "We must help each other out." He spoke about the need to form a cleanup committee and get the young kids in the neighborhood involved. He said it was critical that there be representatives from each block at these meetings.

A white woman, who was a thirty–year resident of the area, told us of her experiences with the block club in her area. She said her block was "fantastic." She said that when it snows, a black man who lives on the block goes up one side of the street and then down the other clearing the snow with his snowblower. Another black resident urged an elderly white neighbor not to move when her children insisted the neighborhood was not safe. He offered to do house maintenance for her. The woman moved to the suburbs, however, and was then quite miserable. She missed her parish and things were no longer accessible by foot. The long–time resident concluded her description of her block by noting that the blacks on her block "don't want an all-black block either."

These vignettes taken from NAO meetings point to the efforts of black and white residents in the area to work on issues of mutual concern. Maintaining the quality of local life, improving security, and reducing crime were interests that they shared. They also had shared concerns about racial steering, panic peddling, mortgage redlining, as well as the quality of city services and schools. This is not to say that there also weren't obvious tensions and differences at these meetings. Still, the efforts of younger black family members and older white residents to communicate across racial lines and to work on issues that were mutually experienced were striking.

Besides block clubs and block watches, NAO also focused on a number of other crime prevention efforts during the period of its Ford funding. These included running the CB Patrol, whose operation was somewhat hampered in the spring of 1983 by the theft of the CB equipment from the NAO office; holding a community–wide workshop on gang crime, as well as a community-wide meeting on "drying up" Division Street; taking a local "peep show" to court, with several NAO members representing the community organization in court; and expanding the activities of the Youth Club.

NAO's concern with social change issues was also evident at its 1983 Annual Meeting. The meeting had about 150 participants with whites in the majority, but with a sizeable number of blacks, and to a lesser extent, Hispanics present. The president of NAO recounted some of the year's activities, which included a focus on zoning problems and city services, the creation of a "job" bank, a concern about conventional mortgages and the Community Reinvestment Act, and a fight against "For Sale" signs and "unethical real estate practices like racial steering." He concluded his remarks by saying "We can't have all black or all white."

One of the speakers that evening represented the Illinois Tax Coalition. He blamed the financial mess the state and city found themselves in on Reaganomics. He proposed three courses of action, which included either doing nothing, raising income taxes on individuals, or pursuing tax reform. The latter course, which he supported, involved closing corporate tax loopholes, providing tax relief from unfair taxes on food and medicine, lowering property taxes, increasing individual income tax exemptions, and "uncoupling" from the federal tax codes Reagan had instituted that meant considerably less revenue for the states. His talk was courteously received.

Northeast Austin was an organization that combined a concern about neighborhood maintenance with one about social change. It was attempting to maintain the stability of neighborhood life in the context of changing racial and economic parameters. Block clubs were the strategy by which communication and cooperation across racial lines were pursued. Crime emerged as an organizational focus because of NAO's concern with maintenance and resident participation. Crime problems were seen as one part of larger security issues, issues that were often defined in social justice terms. For NAO, therefore, preserving the neighborhood and pursuing social change were seen as complementary goals.

NAO was also an organization with constrained resources; within these limits, it was attempting to prevent a pattern of racial transition that has marked Chicago neighborhood history. Ford Foundation funding allowed NAO to pursue its various crime prevention activities and build a watch component into its block club strategy. The block club and other security-based programs articulated well with NAO's overall orientation to neighborhood preservation and social change. Illness among key staff members and other unforeseen contingencies, such as three office burglaries, hampered NAO in pursuing its crime prevention activities with full vigor. More staff and other resources would have allowed NAO to make its diverse approach to crime prevention more robust. Whether NAO will be able to stem the tide of neighborhood racial transition remains to be seen; whether it was able to affect how people felt about where they lived and how much control they had over their neighborhood is looked at in chapter 6. What we observed was how NAO perceived the problems of crime and the breakdown of security and what it did to mitigate these problems. Its effort to implement a block watch program is probably best described as moderate. Its approach to block watch was finally shaped by its limited organizational capacity and by an ideology which only partly emphasized neighborhood preservation.

# 5

# The Community Organizations: Back of the Yards Neighborhood Council, Edgewater Community Council, and Auburn–Gresham Community Action Coalition

The Back of the Yards Neighborhood Council (BYNC) had little affinity for a block watch program, and its effort to implement one can best be described as moderate. The Council was established in 1939, making it one of the oldest existing community organizations in the country. It is an "organization of organizations," composed of 185 local groups. The Council serves an area on the south central side of Chicago, bounded by the Stevenson Expressway on the north, Garfield Boulevard on the south, Racine on the east, and Western Avenue on the west. The area, with small row houses and flats, has a decidedly "working class" flavor. This is also an area that has been undergoing a transformation in the last decade. Ten years ago, this was virtually an all–white community. Now, 65 percent of its residents are white, 7 percent are black, and 28 percent are other non–white individuals. In addition, 48 percent of the community identifies itself as of Hispanic origin. The unemployment rate is 12 percent, and 18 percent of the community lives below the poverty line. About 40 percent of the population is now under twenty years of age and 23 percent of the households are headed by females. About one–third of the residents live in owner–occupied dwellings (Local Community Fact Book, 1984).

The founder of the Council, Joseph Meegan, served as its first executive secretary until his retirement in 1982. Saul Alinsky was also instrumental in the Council's founding. It provided him with the opportunity to combine the tactics of union organizing with the advocacy and service dimensions of social work. The Back of the Yards area was then considered, according to a Council pamphlet, "a hotbed of juvenile delinquency, ill health, poor housing, and social disorganization." The Council was formed

59

in order to unite the separate ethnic, religious, and political factions in the area behind a common goal of wresting a fairer distribution of "values" from the existing powers that be. As Alinsky (1946) himself noted about the Council, "Then they stood and fought as the David of equality for all mankind against the Goliath of prejudice, segregation, and the repression of the prevailing Have's." Alinsky and Bishop Shiel were considered the movers behind the Council's efforts to get food to striking stockyard workers during that period, the same stock yards that were the subject of Upton Sinclair's *The Jungle.*

Nonetheless, the present leaders of Back of the Yards were not eager to claim Alinsky as one of their founders. As the current executive secretary of the Council put it, "It was a different Alinsky than you probably know of—in those days he wasn't radical at all—it was an inner organization, not a city–wide issue type of thing." For his part, Alinsky also had difficulty understanding what the Council had become thirty years after its founding. He said, "They moved into the nightfall of success, and the dreams of achievement which make men fight were replaced by the restless nightmare of fear: fear of change, fear of losing material possessions. Today they are part of the city establishment and are desperately trying to keep their community unchanged" (Alinsky, 1946).

Over the years, the Council has had many success stories, some national and some local. It pioneered the National/State School Lunch and Milk Program, worked for the successful fluoridation of Chicago's water, campaigned for parking meters in Chicago's community shopping areas, sponsored English classes for new residents and adult education classes in citizenship, reading, math, Spanish and Polish, established and financed a center for senior citizens in Back of the Yards, and sponsored summer school programs in reading, math, art, music and physical education for all school children from twenty–nine public and non–public schools. Many of these efforts are ongoing.

The slogan of the Back of the Yards Neighborhood Council is, "We the people will work out our own destiny." The Council considers itself "a grass–roots organization" although it is actually an "organization of organizations." The Council's logo pictures a worker, a priest, and a businessman arm in arm in front of a skyline of manufacturing plants and skyscrapers. The current Executive Secretary explained that the purpose of the Council is to "bring in every church, fraternal, and civic organization in the area so they could all benefit the community. We have always been for the health and welfare of the community, we are not like other community groups— not one issue—but many—employment, counseling, senior citizens, health programs, etc." He added, "There is no problem we don't tackle." Summing up the Council's philosophy he said, "We feel very strongly that accentuating the positive eliminates the negative." The Council in the past was concerned with bringing needed resources and services to a poor and disorganized area. Now its focus was on "preserving" the quality of life that the neighborhood presently enjoyed. This required a very active building upkeep program, strong links to political and other downtown institutions, and programs targeted at particular population groups, such as seniors and juveniles.

The Council was comprised of 185 church, business, labor, social, fraternal, national, educational, recreational, and other organizations. Almost any organization within the Back of the Yards area or which served the citizens of the Back of the Yards could become a Council member. There were no membership dues or charges for services. Each organization sent a delegate and alternative to the Council. At the Annual Community Congress each year, delegates voted for the twenty–four–member Executive Board and a number of policy resolutions. The Executive Board members served one–year terms. The Board also included the vice presidents who headed the seven principal committees: Employment, Juvenile Welfare, Mothers (which included Health and Welfare and Junior Citizens), Conservation, Senior Citizens, Recreation, and Education. The Board included prominent Council members, people important both in the local area and in the larger arena of city politics and business. They met twice a year, while the committees met monthly. There were also monthly Council meetings which were largely informational and social. The turnout at these meetings was usually quite high, especially when well–known public figures were invited to address Council members.

At the time of this study, the Council had seven full–time staff members, two part–time workers and two to ten regular volunteer workers. The Council's budget for FY82 was $183,000 and was projected at $223,000 for FY83. Besides the Ford grant, the Council received a $40,000 grant from United Way. The rest of its treasury was raised privately, through such events as the Annual Fundraising Dinner, the Back of the Yards County Fair and the social events of member organizations. The current executive secretary of the organization was Charles Rycroft. He had been a member of the Council for twenty–seven years and became executive secretary in February 1982. The Council published a weekly newspaper called *The Back of the Yards Journal,* which carried news of Council and other local events.

The Council was involved in a variety of programs which were overseen by its Committees. The Employment Committee provided a free employment service for local residents. The Juvenile Welfare Committee focused on the prevention and treatment of juvenile delinquency. This included counseling sessions for youthful offenders where a parent, youth officer, and Council staff member were present. About 115 young people were seen each month. The Conservation Committee focused on the physical upkeep of the area, particularly the removal of abandoned cars, helped in building new homes and remodeling old ones, and monitored existing houses for code compliance. The Mother's Committee was concerned with the health and welfare of area residents and was also involved in activities with area youth. The Senior Citizen's Committee and Council staff monitored fourteen senior citizens clubs and made information available about housing, health, and medical services. The Education Committee consisted of twenty–seven principals from public and parochial schools in Back of the Yards who were kept informed about city and Council services. The Recreation Committee worked closely with the Park District to assure that the area's facilities were adequately used and maintained.

Crime was a concern of local residents. According to our survey, almost 33 percent of the residents in the area targeted for block watch at Time 1 thought that crime had increased in the neighborhood over the last year, compared to 17 percent of the Chicago city sample. Still, the Council's approach of "accentuating the positive" moved it in the direction of providing programs that focused on the *causes* of the problem, rather than simply "reducing victimizations." This meant a concern with unemployment, preventing and treating juvenile delinquency, maintaining the area's physical integrity, and providing adequate educational and recreational opportunities for young people. The executive secretary of the Council stated, "We're not a high crime area; we're an area that has crime problems." He pointed out that "adult–incidence of crime perpetrated by residents is not very high; primarily it is of a youth nature." The Council did have an Urban Crime Prevention Program which was funded under the original grant from LEAA. The focus of the program was on vandalism, graffiti, property damage, and shoplifting. These were ongoing concerns of the Council.

Under Ford Foundation funding, Back of the Yards expanded its ongoing crime prevention efforts while adding a block watch component. The crime project director for Back of the Yards was Ben Mecray, a young man in his mid–twenties who worked for the Council under the LEAA grant. Ben had a BA in Criminal Justice and had worked as a private investigator for an insurance company. He was the only paid staff member who worked on crime, and he relied on volunteers from the Council to carry out the program.

In the first year of the program, Ben, in consultation with the executive director, established his program goals. Forty–five percent of program time was focused on block watch, which included door–to–door work (30 percent) and presentations to senior citizens' groups (15 percent). Another 20 percent of his time was devoted to youth and schools, including juvenile welfare counseling and presentations to sixth, seventh, and eighth graders in the area on graffiti, vandalism, and shoplifting. An additional 20 percent of the program was directed at businesses in the area, especially those in the Back of the Yards Businessmen's Association. Ten percent of the program was aimed at the park supervisors and regular visits Ben would make. Finally, the remaining 5 percent of the program was directed at existing groups in the Council, such as the Mother's Committee and the Employment Committee. During that first year, Ben chose a thirty–nine–block target area in which he hoped to establish twenty block watches. In the second year of Ford funding, Ben raised the portion of the program devoted to juvenile welfare and business visits. He also set a goal of seventeen more block watches within the same target area he had the first year.

From January through July 1983, Ben established eleven watches and recruited eleven block representatives. He also made regular visits to businesses in the area to see what security problems they were having, met regularly with park supervisors, made presentations to senior groups about crime and security, made other presentations to groups like the Mother's Committee and sixth, seventh, and eighth graders, and held counseling sessions with young offenders. From August 1983 through February 1984, Ben established six more block watches, recruited six block representatives, and continued the other aspects of his crime prevention activities.

Ben's target area was 58 percent white, 4 percent non–white individuals, and 38 percent Hispanic. Ben said it was hardest for him to get Hispanics to attend the meetings; most of the participants were white. When Ben began organizing watches, he generally held the block meetings in a nearby park. He found that people were reluctant to open their homes to people they didn't know. They were also reluctant to exchange phone numbers. After meeting with CIS consultant Jack Houck, Ben started to make greater use of the churches in the area to advertise the program and said he was having more success in getting people to open up their homes for meetings.

When we asked residents in the target area at Time 1 whether they felt part of their neighborhood or thought of it more as a place to live, 58 percent said they felt a part of the neighborhood, compared to 61 percent of the Chicago city sample. However, when we asked what they thought the neighborhood would be like two years from now, almost 41 percent said they thought it would be worse, as compared to 15 percent of the Chicago city sample.

Ben kept up regular contacts with the block representatives he recruited. He would visit with them or speak to them on the phone. The reps generally reported on what was going on on their blocks and saw Ben as a link to greater control and responsiveness. It was not clear, however, that block reps necessarily saw *their* role as providing other people on their blocks with greater security. There were some block residents they might turn to, but it appeared that Ben was their real link to security. One rep made it clear that it was her neighbors whom she feared, while another described to Ben an attack on a man walking down the street where the rep not only did not call her neighbor, she did not call the police. Ben credited one of the watches he established, however, with shutting down two taverns that were serving liquor to minors.

One block watch meeting we did attend in Back of the Yards took place in a home on a block other than the one where the meeting participants lived. Although a phone tree was established and Ben handed out a lot of information about home security and other safety tips, an underlying theme to the meeting was that it was difficult to trust anyone these days. Whether the meeting resulted in participants feeling they now had more control over the events on their block was not clear, but one of the messages seemed to be that in the world–at–large, things were greatly out of control.

At his presentations other than block watch, Ben's purpose was largely educational. Whether at a Mother's Committee meeting or a senior citizens club, Ben first established the nature of the crime problem that affected that group and then discussed various ways they could deal with it. He talked about the block watch, but since the participants at these meetings did not all live on the same block, Ben left it up to them to contact him if they wanted to start a watch. His purpose was to let them know that the Council was involved in such a program and he was available to help if they needed it.

At Ben's school visits, he discussed the seriousness of such offenses as graffiti, vandalism, and shoplifting with the students. His purpose in visiting local businesses was to find out if any unusual crimes had gone on and to see that the local police department was responsive to the merchants. Ben said he enjoyed excellent relations with the local police department, sat on its Steering Committee, and thought highly of the Neighborhood Relations Sergeant and Beat Rep. He said that he only requested monthly statistics from the local police department.

One monthly Council meeting we attended had the Superintendent of the Chicago Police Department and the head of the Gangs Crime unit as featured speakers. They appeared highly professional and sophisticated, while trying to remain open and sensitive to the needs of ordinary citizens. Attracting such luminaries to its monthly meeting made the Council leadership look influential and effective to local residents.

Several factors shaped the Back of the Yards approach to dealing with crime in its area. There was first the ideological emphasis on "accentuating" the positive and focusing on the social or economic causes of such criminal activity. Reducing victimizations was not critical to this approach.

Second was the structural fact that the Council was an organization of organizations. Its constituents were member organizations, not individuals. The Council was therefore not motivated to organize individuals massively on the block level as an all–out block watch effort would require. Indeed such an endeavor might undermine the Council's structure of substantive committees.

Third, the Council at this stage in its development had strong linkages to the political and governmental institutions it sought to influence. This meant it tried to provide services to key constituencies, such as seniors, businessmen, and juveniles and relied on its influence with existing institutions, whether the police or City Hall, to get "action" on local problems that needed attention.

The Back of the Yards Neighborhood Council ran a comprehensive crime prevention program, one that fit with *its* general philosophy and approach to organizing. Its approach to crime prevention, however, was not especially compatible with a block watch strategy. It was instead focused on education, service, and institutional responsiveness. The Council did not really have an interest in "alternative" crime prevention strategies or "alternative" organizing strategies. Its goal was to continue its own approaches and strategies, which it had utilized successfully over the past forty–seven years. The Council was no longer "social change"–oriented as it was in its founding days, although it retained some of the ideological trappings of those days; now it was focused on preservation and maintenance of its hard–won privileges. Though now oriented to neighborhood preservation, the Council's structure was not conducive to the amplification of individual resident concerns. While local crime was an issue the Council could not ignore, a block watch program was not useful to the Council for recruiting members or for pursuing its political goals. In fact, in many ways, the Council's leadership probably saw this approach to crime prevention as counterproductive to its basic interests.

## The Edgewater Community Council

The Edgewater Community Council (ECC) made a weak effort to implement a block watch program. ECC was formed in 1961. Its membership includes individuals, block clubs, and other local organizations. ECC serves an area on Chicago's north side that is bordered by Devon on the north, Foster on the south, the lake on the east, and Ravenswood on the west. The area is ethnically diverse; its population is 72 percent white, 11 percent black, and 17 percent other non–white individuals. About 13 percent of the area's residents identify themselves as of Hispanic origin. Eleven percent of the population lives below the poverty line, while 7 percent are unemployed. Twenty–six percent of the households are headed by females and 21 percent of the population is below twenty years of age. Only 23 percent of the residents live in owner–occupied dwellings (Local Community Fact Book, 1984).

Edgewater is a community with at least three sub–communities. There is the area of new high–rise and luxury apartment buildings which border the lakefront. There is also the central strip in the community (Kenmore–Winthrop) which has older apartment buildings, many of which serve as transient and residential hotels, as well as low–income and medium–income rental units. Finally, there is the section west of Broadway that consists largely of single family homes and two and three flats.

The Edgewater Community Council was founded by local businessmen, clergy, and community activists who "needed some organization to speak for the community." Its leadership believes that "ECC acts as a sounding board for ideas and provides the leadership necessary to plan innovatively for Edgewater's future." Although it has been concerned with many local issues over the years, the Council was especially concerned within the last ten years with the housing decline along the Kenmore–Winthrop strip, an area that the city of Chicago declared a Neighborhood Strategy Area, making it eligible for federal redevelopment funds. The Council has also been concerned with the appearance of video arcades, massage parlors, and liquor stores along Broadway, a major thoroughfare in the area. The diversity of the area produced a diversity of constituencies seeking to affect the Council's actions. There were the more well–to–do residents along the lakefront, who were in some ways encapsulated in their highrises, but who were nonetheless concerned about crime and security and maintaining the quality of the lakefront. There were the poorer and more transient residents along the Kenmore–Winthrop strip, many of whom were not involved in Council activities but whose interests one can assume would be along "social justice" lines, underscoring the need to bring more resources to an impoverished area. West of Broadway were homeowners concerned with a variety of issues like the quality of city services and city schools, and the need to improve security and reduce crime. There was, thus, an underlying tension on the Council between those who had a "preservation" orientation and saw crime and security as central issues, those with a "social justice" orientation who wanted a better distribution of values, and those with a "social change" orientation who wanted to upgrade the area and downplay the negative image concern which crime created (often, young, white, urban professionals). The Council developed a variety of programs to deal with the needs of its various constituencies.

The Council had about 1200 members. To be a member, individuals paid $7.50 a year, families paid $15.00 and seniors paid $4.00. Any dues–paying member could vote in Council elections. The Council had a thirty–seven–member Board of Directors. Elections were held for thirty seats on the Board plus seven officers. Board members served three–year terms; officers were elected annually. The Board met on a monthly basis. There was also a ten–member Executive Committee, which included the seven officers of the Council as well as the chairs of the Planning and Development and Publicity Committees. Other important Council committees were the Finance Committee, the Personal Safety Committee, the Conservation and Housing Committee, and the Care–for–Real Committee. The Council had four full–time staff members and three part–time members. The executive director of the Council was Bill Meskanski. The budget of the Council for FY83 was $160,000. The Ford Foundation crime project contributed to that total.

The Council operated a number of programs. One key program was Operation Kenmore–Winthrop through which "ECC seeks to improve housing in the community by encouraging responsible investment by owners and developers." The Council received a $20,000 grant from the city of Chicago to run this project. The Council also sponsored Operation Lakewatch in order "to preserve as much open land on the lakefront as possible and to protect the beaches and lake recreation areas from pollution." The Council was also involved in increasing recreational areas for public use, which included negotiations over the "Viatorium" and "Armory" properties with city and federal agencies. The Council sponsored Care–for–Real, which served as a food pantry, clothing distribution, and referral service for the area's poor and needy. Finally, the Council founded the WHISTLESTOP Program, which had distributed 300,000 WHISTLEPACS since 1973; and it participated in the Urban Crime Prevention Program as a response to local concerns about crime and security.

The Edgewater Community Council was one of the original groups that received funds from LEAA to do community crime prevention. The Council used its LEAA funding primarily for an arson prevention program in the Kenmore–Winthrop area. The Edgewater Council then began receiving funds from the Ford Foundation to continue its crime prevention efforts under the CIS umbrella. The director of the crime prevention program under LEAA funding and Ford funding was Jim Short. In addition to Jim, there was a half–time Council staff member, a student intern from Loyola University, and a VISTA volunteer who worked on the crime program, as well as volunteers from the Council. Jim reported to both the Personal Safety Committee and the Council's Board of Directors on program activities.

Jim believed there were two aspects to the crime problem in the Edge-water area. The first was the problem of the "perception" of crime. Because people were fearful, there were unfortunate responses, such as staying off the streets at night. Jim pointed out that "people who perpetrate crime don't want witnesses." He said the Council wanted to get "people's fear level down to a controllable point—as long as it's controllable fear, where people understand they can do something about their own problem, then we're on our way."

The other aspect to the crime problem was the presence of "social mal-adjustees" out on the streets in the Edgewater area. Jim pointed out that the presence of these persons creates "victims," as people respond fearfully or seek to isolate themselves. Jim said that in Edgewater both the potential for crime and the fear of crime existed. Under their LEAA grant, they had directed most of their efforts east of Broadway, particularly in the Ken-more–Winthrop area. Under Ford funding, Jim proposed directing their efforts west of Broadway, while keeping up maintenance efforts in the Kenmore–Winthrop area.

Jim's goals under the Ford funding were to establish twenty–five block watches within five block club areas. The five block clubs were: Every Person Is Concerned (EPIC); Edgewater Triangle Neighbors Association; West Andersonville Neighbors Together (WANT); Lakewood–Balmoral Residents Council; and Kenmore–Winthrop Residents. Three of the block clubs had housing concerns, a focus both the Council and Jim had gained experience with under their LEAA funding. Jim proposed that target build-ing become a focus for block watches. He saw the purpose of the watch being "to bring people together to allow people to know each other." Phone trees could then be established. Jim also hoped to market "VAL–U–GUARD" engraving kits as part of their crime prevention efforts, which would also provide a source of matching funds for their grant.

According to our survey, 79 percent of the residents in the target area were white, 11 percent were Asian, almost 5 percent were Hispanic, and 3 percent were other non–white individuals. When we asked residents in the target area at Time 1 whether they felt a part of their neighborhood, 69.3 percent said they did, compared to 61 percent of the Chicago city sample. When we asked what they thought the neighborhood would be like in two years, 24.5 percent said it would be better, compared to 25 percent of the Chicago city sample, and 58.4 percent said it would be about the same, compared to 59.5 percent of the Chicago city sample. When we asked about the amount of crime in the neighborhood over the past year, 67 percent said it had stayed about the same, compared to 70.8 percent of the Chicago city sample.

Under Jim's tenure as crime project director from August 1982 through

October 1983, one block watch was established. Jim claimed to have established six other watches in April and May of 1983. This claim was denied by the replacement director of the Edgewater Community Council crime program, by the executive director of the Council, and by the president of the Edgewater Council during 1983. All three told us that only one watch was established in the fall of 1983, and that was in the Lakewood–Balmoral area after neighborhood residents asked for Jim's assistance following a series of break-ins in the neighborhood.

Several factors account for the poor showing of the Edgewater Community Council in establishing block watches. The Council and Jim Short had gained a lot of expertise and results through Housing Court under their LEAA grant. Their highly praised arson program had been directly linked to the Operation Kenmore–Winthrop program, one that the Council valued very much. Jim had supervised the Housing Court work under the program and was "an all-purpose trouble-shooter" according to the executive director of the Council in 1983. He noted, "Jim could take a building all the way through Housing Court, mediate with a bank, negotiate with people."

However, in establishing the objectives for their program under Ford funding, Jim proposed, in consultation with some Board members and CIS staff, to focus their crime prevention efforts west of Broadway. Both the executive director of the Council and the 1983 Board president commented to us how this new focus was a "constraining factor" because the real need for security measures was still in the Kenmore–Winthrop area. Jim himself did not agree with this analysis. He said there was a lot of organizational support for Operation Kenmore–Winthrop, which helped to make the arson program such a success. But Jim also felt there was denial about the crime problems west of Broadway. The 1983 president of the Council, commenting on the rash of crime problems that occurred in the Lakewood–Balmoral area (which is west of Broadway) in the fall of 1983, said that despite the incidents in Lakewood–Balmoral, he did not think it was a high crime area. He said, "Sure, incidents happen, as they do everywhere. True, too, that 144 people came out to the meeting in the Lakewood–Balmoral area. Still, I don't think that crime really is a problem there."

Differences on the Board over the priorities that should be given to crime and security problems added to the eventual ineffectiveness of the crime program which Jim had proposed. But even before these conflicts had their consequences, a predominant factor in the weakness of Edgewater's program was that Jim Short was not a trained community organizer. His skills, as noted above, had been honed in Housing Court battles and were more suited to "brokering power" among different interests in the community.

The 1983 Council president said "His skills didn't plug in. He was not an organizer, although he was good at intimidating slumlords and was good with rhetoric." The 1983 executive director agreed. He said Jim was out on the streets; he could deal well with various constituent complaints. "But he really wasn't an organizer."

For his part, Jim felt stymied by the "population density" in the areas he had to organize and by the lack of resources and support from the Council. He said, "The area from Foster to Devon and from the El to the lake is the fourth largest city in Illinois—20,000 people live in twenty-four square blocks." Jim complained that getting 25 percent of a block to attend a meeting on some of the blocks he was trying to organize meant getting 250 people to a meeting. A compromise was eventually worked out with CIS to define something called a "block network," which would require only 15 percent of the households on a block to sign up on a phone tree. These never materialized, however.

Even where population density was not so much a factor, Jim had trouble getting people to turn out to meetings. Jim organized an areawide Crime Prevention meeting in May 1983 to draw the community's attention to the Council's block watch program and other safety programs. The meeting hall was set up with about 100 chairs, but only eight people showed up. A well-orchestrated program had been planned, which included a talk by a crime reporter from the Chicago *Tribune,* a talk by Arthur Sims of CIS on the community crime prevention "movement," and a talk by Jim about block watch, VAL–U–GUARD, and a new door–lock system. Many of the Council's officers and committee chairs were present, but the average citizens of the community were not there. The "people" were not there.

We went to the offices of the Edgewater Council in late June 1983 to attend a meeting of residents of the Edgewater Triangle area. No one showed up for the meeting. At a postmortem discussion about why no one had showed up, the two young women volunteers who had gone door–to–door talked about the high level of fear that people had in the neighborhood, that some did not even want to open their doors. Still, they felt there was interest and that there needed to be follow–up. The president of the Triangle Block Club was present, and he pointed out that many of the area's residents were seniors who did not feel safe venturing east of Broadway to attend a meeting in the council's office in the evening. He suggested that a local church would be a better site for a neighborhood meeting.

By the summer of 1983, Jim felt great frustration because he was not getting support from the Council's Board to run the program properly. He had expected the Council to raise and allot matching funds for the program. Even when some Board members tried to help, there was no way to earmark the money specifically for the crime program. Jim said even "in kind" amenities like postage become a hassle.

The Board president and the executive director were also frustrated about Jim and the program. The executive director told us that members of the Finance Committee expected Jim to raise the matching funds needed for the grant, while Jim was waiting for them to raise it. He pointed out that the program got off to a bad start under Ford monies, first because of the hiatus in funding and secondly because of antagonism between the outgoing president of the Council in 1982 and Jim. Moreover, the executive director felt that Jim had not been good at defining realistic objectives for the program under Ford Foundation funding. He added that the Board "never realistically assessed Jim's continuation proposal to Ford."

The question of what to do about the program and about Jim came before the Council's Board several times, but no clear resolution to act came forth. On the one hand, the executive director felt it was the Board's responsibility to do something. The Board, however, found it hard to act because of Jim's roots in the community and the effective job he had done with the arson program. When Jim's request for a salary increase could not be met in the Fall of 1983, Jim himself decided to leave his job. In September, however, he was able to assist the members of the Lakewood–Balmoral Residents' Council to set up a block watch in their area and it was hoped that several more block watches in that area would result.

Jim was replaced as crime project director by George Baum who had handled the bulk of housing court work for Jim under the Ford funding. The Council reduced staff positions for the crime program to one full–time position from one and one–half positions and was then able to bring its program budget back into the black. George officially became the new crime project director in December 1983. George told us that he would be working under the objectives that Jim had established and was going to focus his first efforts in the Triangle area, followed then by efforts in the EPIC area.

We did attend a meeting of residents in the Triangle area that George organized at the Edgewater Baptist Church in late February 1984. About seventy–five people were present at the meeting. Speakers included theNeighborhood Relations Sergeant from the 20th Police District, the Edgewater Council's representative to the CIS Steering Committee, the chair of the Council's Personal Safety Committee, a volunteer who helped to organize the meeting, a representative from the Lakewood Balmoral Residents Council, and the local alderperson. George had the participants break up into small groups at the end of the meeting and assemble under signs that indicated the streets on which they lived. George saw this as organizing the nucleus for block watches on those blocks.

The outgoing Board president expressed to us his feelings about the usefulness of "block networks" and the Board's continuing commitment to the crime program. The executive director said their goals now would be "to meet the objectives of the crime program as quickly as possible." He said they needed to use their limited resources to stay visible west of Broadway, especially in Triangle, EPIC, and Barge. He concluded by saying that "organizing was important to the organization, getting people involved in programs, getting more minority representation."

The Edgewater Community Council had several constituencies which defined crime and security concerns in different ways. To those with a "social change" orientation, the redevelopment of Kenmore–Winthrop was central, while to those with a "preservation" orientation, the reduction of "victimizations" was key. The third constituency, not as active in the Edgewater Council as in other local community organizations, was more concerned with "social justice" and bringing needed economic and social resources into the area.

There had been a consensus on the Council about the objectives of Operation Kenmore–Winthrop. It met the needs of the three major Council constituencies. The Council's arson program, run with LEAA funds, was directly linked to Operation Kenmore–Winthrop and helps to explain that program's success. The new goals for the crime program under Ford Foundation funding were never fully assessed by the Board in conjunction with program staff. This resulted in lack of support for the program, which was compounded by the program director's lack of community organizing experience. What resulted was an ineffectual block watch program, although Housing Court efforts still continued in full force, efforts which many Board members saw as one of the linchpins of local security.

Although block watch was a potential source of new members and met some of the Council's political development needs, its poor implementation could be tolerated because the Council was presently robust enough to insure membership gains and political development from other sources. Moreover, a full–fledged effort to implement a block watch program would probably have been too costly in terms of competing constituency and ideological orientations within the Council. Though concerned about crime and neighborhood preservation, the Council's leadership saw only limited benefits in implementing a comprehensive block watch program.

## The Auburn–Gresham Community Action Coalition

The effort of the Auburn–Gresham Community Action Coalition (AGCAC) to implement a block watch program, like that of Edgewater Community Council, was weak. AGCAC was founded in 1977. It serves an area on Chicago's south side bordered by 75th Street on the north, 95th Street on the south, the Dan Ryan Expressway on the east and Western

Avenue on the west. It is an organization composed of individuals, block clubs, and various local groups.

This is a solid black community on the south side of the city. Ten years ago, 69 percent of its residents were black; today that figure is 98 percent. Almost half of those employed are in white collar occupations. Thirteen percent of the residents are unemployed and the same percentage is living below the poverty line. This represents increases over the last ten years. The percentage of female–headed households also increased significantly over the same period, moving from 17 percent to 36 percent of the households. In addition, almost 40 percent of the current residents are below the age of twenty.

About half the homes in this area are owner–occupied. These homes are modest, but well–kept single–family dwellings which front on tree–lined streets. Some of the main streets in the area, such as Ashland Avenue, show signs of "incivilities." At the same time, there is also evidence of surviving small businesses and other commercial activity, including two local banks.

AGCAC was founded over the issue of insurance redlining in the area and why homeowners could not obtain insurance. The founding members of the Coalition were local residents who received help from an organizer from the National Training and Information Center. The Coalition helped to secure the passage of a state insurance plan called the Fair Plan and then went on to secure a commitment from Allstate Insurance Company to review and reduce its nonrenewal rate for Auburn–Gresham homeowners and to invest over $1 million back into the south and west sides of Chicago. AGCAC was still involved in the process of implementing those redevelopment plans.

An AGCAC brochure described the goals of the organization as seeking to "involve area residents, business people, and organizations in maintaining and revitalizing the community and in obtaining solutions to other community problems." According to one of its founding members, the Auburn–Gresham Community Action Coalition was "concerned with building leadership in the community, creating stability for future generations, and reinvesting in the community." Besides the issue of insurance redlining, AGCAC has also turned its attention to utility reform and advocacy, housing issues, education, health care, crime, commercial revitalization, and city services. This same founding member, now a Board member, noted that the organization was concerned with "helping people to help themselves." She added that "people learn to speak out, to stand up and talk to presidents of insurance companies, presidents of banks, officials of HUD. It is a growth process."

The organization had a twenty–member Board of Directors who were elected at a mini–Congress for two–year terms. Candidates could run as part of a slate. At the time of our study, there was an active core of six Board members who formed the leadership of the organization. The Board president was Leslie Turner. The Board met on a monthly basis. Any dues-paying member (dues were $4.00 per year) could vote in elections. Although the exact membership total was not known, there was a core of 100 active Coalition members. One hundred block clubs also existed in the area. General Coalition meetings were held about every two months. Outside of the crime program director, there was no paid staff. Auburn–Gresham did have a VISTA worker and a group of ten volunteer workers. The annual budget of AGCAC was $66,000 raised from membership fees, donations, and grants.

AGCAC was concerned with a number of local issues and problems. It was active in the effort to bring reforms to utility services in the state, particularly in the area of overcharges and cut–offs. It also maintained a focus on local housing problems and monitored how federal Community Development Block Grants were spent and supported the development of block clubs to act on abandoned buildings and other hazardous neighborhood sites. AGCAC was concerned with local commercial revitalization and helped to create the Auburn–Gresham Business Association. It was also concerned with the quality of local education, the availability of preventive health care, the improvement of city services, and the effort to reduce crime and increase local security.

There were at least two motivating forces behind AGCAC's concern with local crime and security. There was the basic desire to maintain "control" over the neighborhood and to make it a place where people wanted to live and be involved in its upkeep. There was also the relationship between crime rates and the availability of insurance and other financial opportunities. The leadership of AGCAC hoped that by lowering the crime rate in the area, residents would be better able to secure home loans, mortgages, and insurance with less trouble and at more reasonable rates than they had in the past.

The Auburn–Gresham Community Action Coalition was part of the original group that received crime prevention funding from LEAA. A founding member of the Coalition said that at one time, "the neighborhood was up for grabs." There was a real problem with gangs and home invasions. She said that local businessmen and others got together with two watch commanders to help identify trouble spots. Under the Urban Crime Prevention Program, they began to establish block watches, post area alert signs, paint numbers on the backs of garages so they could be spotted more easily by the police, and use engraving pens to mark valuables. Sixty–four blocks were organized with these funds. The VISTA volunteer who worked on the UCPP and was instrumental in its success was Frieda Green. She told us that they would go into an area and set up a block club if one did not already exist. The block watch then was added on. She said that they would stay with a block club until "they get on their own feet—we always follow-up." She added that it was often necessary to take care of other problems first—such as an abandoned building or someone's not having enough food to eat.

Frieda told of one block where a house burned down and where there had been other fires as well. They worked with block residents and the police to take care of housing violations. She said that block stood on its own now, and there have not been further fires. She also talked of meeting a young woman who did not have enough food to feed herself and her baby—"she was a broken, hurt woman." AGCAC helped to get her food and get her involved in the organization. "Now she is a strong community person—she is now organizing from the heart." She helped to organize five block clubs where she lived.

AGCAC also was part of the umbrella that received money from the Ford Foundation to continue its crime prevention efforts in August 1982. AGCAC experienced a hiatus in its program when its program director left at the end of LEAA funding. In late fall 1982, AGCAC hired Terry Joseph as its new crime project director. Terry had been an organizer with The Woodlawn Organization in 1972–73 and had received further training and experience in community organizing and board development with the National Urban League. Terry saw one of his major goals to be contacting existing block clubs and reinitiating dormant ones in his target area. Terry was also aware that there were any number of issues that might concern the community. He noted, "If they have a need and we can give them some assistance, we're gonna do it." Crime might therefore be only one among a variety of problems that residents had. Terry also saw the need to link crime statistics and insurance rates and so saw the effort to get accurate and regular crime statistics from the local police department as critical. Terry also believed there was a definite connection between unemployment, inadequate education, and crime.

The area targeted for the block watch program was 95 percent black, 3 percent white and 2 percent other non–white individuals. When we asked residents in the area at Time 1 whether they felt a part of their neighborhood or thought of it as just a place to live, an overwhelming 84.3 percent said they felt a part of their neighborhood (as compared to 61 percent of the Chicago city sample). When we asked them what their neighborhood would be like in two years, 30 percent said they thought it would be better (compared to 25 percent of the city sample) and 64 percent said they thought it would be the same (compared to 59.5 percent of the city sample). When we asked if the amount of crime had increased in the last year, 70.4 percent said it had stayed the same (70.8 percent of the city sample gave that response) and 18.1 percent said it had decreased (12.1 percent of the city sample gave that response).

Terry quit his post as crime project director for the Auburn–Gresham Community Action Coalition in June 1983. He told us that at that point he had organized four block watches and one floor of a Chicago Housing Authority apartment building. (We were never able to observe any crime prevention meetings during our fifteen months in the field, however.) Terry said he ran into several problems that had hampered his ability to carry out his crime program goals.

He was the only paid staff member at the organization which meant that he needed to recruit volunteers to help him with his organizing work. He had gotten together some volunteers to help him on "Housing Counseling" and advising homeowners about home improvement loans. He saw this as a foot in the door to getting residents involved in the crime program. But organizing takes a lot of time and effort. In some areas, he first had to organize block clubs, which take longer to establish than just watches. He felt that in black neighborhoods, block clubs were a very accepted form of local organization. The problem was compounded by the lack of internal staff support, which he needed in order to get proposals written to secure matching funds. Terry saw the effort to secure these funds consuming a lot of his time. He said that by the time he left, he felt AGCAC was close to making its match. AGCAC had failed to file certain tax papers with the IRS, however, and so it could not receive its matching funds until those papers had been processed. This meant that the program would be out of money by the end of its 1983 fiscal year. Since Terry could not work without salary for two to three months, he was forced to quit. In addition, he felt that the Board of the organization needed to be built up and he did not have the time nor did he think it was his responsibility to take on that task. These factors all figured into his decision to leave, although it was finally the lack of funds that forced him to quit.

At a meeting of the Board of Directors in April 1983, Gladys Jones and Arthur Sims of CIS came to AGCAC to discuss the process of building a coalition of the community organizations receiving Ford funding as a vehicle to continue their efforts after that funding ended. Gladys talked about the coalition building process, but then stopped and talked about her concerns that AGCAC could not make their match and that there was not enough "Board" to keep the organization running adequately. There was a heated response to Gladys' remarks from the five Board members present. One expressed the idea that they did not just represent themselves, but represented the whole neighborhood and all the groups in it. Thus, a small Board did not mean that they were not representative or needed in the area. Pointing to the head of the Auburn–Gresham Business Association, one Board member said, "He doesn't just represent himself. He represents twenty others, and we started that Association." Another added, "We have something to offer. We have the support of local politicians." He later said, "We're a real grassroots organization. In fact, we're below the grass. We're the dirt."

One frustrated Board member and a founding member of AGCAC said that in order to receive the Ford monies, CIS had put a lot of demands on their organization. She said, "CIS takes up all your goddam time and it don't give you anything. Every time the phone rings, it's CIS. $17,792 ain't no money." Another added that CIS "wasn't really concerned about the community organization's problems."

Because of their concern with Auburn–Gresham's ability to make match, to build up an adequate Board, and to meet their crime program objectives, CIS told the Auburn–Gresham Community Action Coalition that it was coming under a review. With the departure of Terry Joseph as crime project director, the leaders of AGCAC decided that they would withdraw from the crime program rather than come under review. They withdrew from the program in late June 1983.

At an interview in September 1983 with Leslie Turner, a board member of AGCAC, he expressed the hope that Auburn–Gresham would be on the upswing again soon. He felt that organizations go through cycles and that AGCAC needed to regroup and bring in some fresh blood. He noted the paradox that AGCAC had a national reputation on insurance and housing issues but did not receive enough credit locally. Leslie felt both the experience with UCPP and the experience they had gained over the years would allow them to get back on track soon.

The Auburn–Gresham Community Action Coalition had a mixture of concerns about "social change" and "preservation." In this organization, the balance tipped toward "social change" and the need to bring resources and services into a "middle–class poor" area. AGCAC had cut its teeth on a number of issue campaigns that placed it in the national eye. The organization was also concerned with building local leadership and finding solutions to local problems. But it seems to have failed, at least in the eyes of CIS, at "rooting itself" in the neighborhood and developing the type of participation that would be needed to maintain the organization and work on "preservation" issues in the neighborhood. For its part, CIS did not appear to be sensitive to the political needs of the organization, and added to the problems of an already weak and resource–poor organization by putting stress on matching funds and by failing to find a means to assist in building up board and membership participation. It was clear that there were crime and security needs in this neighborhood and that the leaders of the organization were concerned about them. This was precisely the type of neighborhood where "security" also needed to be redistributed. For the Auburn–Gresham Community Action Coalition, the costs of participating in the crime prevention program ultimately became too great. The program neither insured increased membership in an organization only partly concerned with "preservation" goals, while the program proved a deflection from the more essential political development needs of the organization.

# 6

# The Impact of Block Watch
# on the Communities

All reform efforts have within them theories of individual action. They each propose, at least implicitly, the conditions under which certain types of behavior will be produced, and how that behavior will be elicited. When the behavior in question is economic, the causal change is often well specified. This is less often the case when the behaviors in question are more social and political. Often the reformers know what behaviors they want to be produced, but they are less clear about describing the possible variations which might be produced. This reticence to describe the unintended behaviors which might occur has as much to do with promoting the reform as it does with the capacity of the social sciences to predict behavior. The selling of a reform depends on the certainty that its promoters have about what the reform will produce. If innovators begin to spell out all the things which might happen, they make the sponsors of such efforts squeamish about the likely payoff of their investment. The more deterministic the presentation, if we do A it will lead to B, the more confident the sponsors can be about what they will get for the effort. Once reformers and social scientists begin to talk about the conditions under which A will lead to B and *how* A and B are related, they undermine their support among sponsors who have many competing demands for their resources, and like to feel they are betting on as sure a thing as possible.

Block watch is no exception. Supporters of the block watch reform argued that if one does block watch, communities will be better off, have less crime and be more cohesive. CIS made the case to Ford, CIS made the case to the community organizations, block watch advocates made the case to others within their community organizations, and block watch organizers made their case to community residents at the meetings which were held to promote the watches.

The sequence of events which had to take place if the result was to be

79

achieved was often left unspecified because at each level of interaction the promoter was trying to get the person committed to the end result, not puzzling over the likelihood of whether the sequence would take place and produce the anticipated outcomes. Ultimately, the test for block watch is how it affects the residents of the communities in which it is tried. Indeed, the last level at which pragmatic interactions take place is between residents of the community who have been involved in the block watch initiative. A field work methodology would be impossible to administer in observing how the five communities in question were changed by the block watch activities. There are simply too many people to observe over too long a period of time. We thus administered a survey at two points in time (before the block watches were started and a year after they were introduced) to randomly selected members of the communities targeted for the program and in communities which were matched to the target areas on the basis of demographic similarities. In this way we could assess how the communities were changed by the introduction of the block watch.

In order for the block watch to work, there is a series of events which has to take place. Each event in that sequence is premised on the antecedent event having taken place first, for the logic of the strategy demands the ordering of the events. Residents of the community must be aware that block watch meetings are happening in their community. They cannot be expected to attend if they do not know that they have that opportunity. Then, they must go to the meetings. This participation is perhaps the most important event in the sequence, for it is at the block watch meeting that the individual is introduced to the activities which are the backbone of the strategy. Second, the participator should change her attitude about the efficacy of personal action in the crime prevention process. Individuals should come away from those meetings or from interaction with people who went to the meetings with an improved sense of what citizens can accomplish to make their communities more secure. They should no longer simply depend on the police for protection.

Third, community residents should change their behavior. As a result of the block meetings and the interactions with neighbors and organizers that follow, residents ought to be doing things differently than they did before the block watches were introduced. In particular, residents should engage in both individual and collective preventive actions and show a new willingness to intervene in neighborhood problems. Fourth, and this is one of the ultimate goals of the block watch, the social integration of residents ought to be improved by the efforts. Interactions with neighbors ought to increase and residents should know more people on their block. Assuming that all five events and processes in this sequence have taken place, we ought to see changes in the community, changes which the block watch

**FIGURE 6-1**
**The Block Watch Transformation Sequence**

Knowledge and Participation in Block Watch (1)

Perceived Efficacy of Citizen Action (2)

New Crime Prevention Behavior Employed (3)

More Awareness of Neighbors (4)

Crime Reduced (5)

Fear Lowered (6)

More Attachment to the Community (7)

---

strategy suggests will follow from implementing the strategy. Thus, fifth, crime and what we call incivilities ought to be reduced. There should be fewer victimizations and there should also be a reduction in the kinds of disorders which the block watches were meant to reduce (e.g., vandalism, graffitti, gang activity, etc.).

Sixth, if all the steps outlined above have been taken, communities with block watch should see a decline in the amount of fear in the community. People will feel less afraid both because they feel more efficacious and because the objective threat in the community has been reduced by the introduction of the block watch. This should lead to the final step in the sequence which is an increase in optimism and attachment to the neighborhood. Residents should feel better about living in the community and have higher hopes for the future of the area.

In this chapter, we treat each step in the block watch sequence as a hypothesis to test with the data we collected from our survey. Figure 6-1 schematizes our discussion. We compare differences between treated and untreated communities over time. We look at differential change over the one–year period between treated and untreated areas. While we cannot observe the interactions between neighbors over the year, this design allows us to analyze the impact of the block watch on the communities which were to be improved. The Appendix at the end of the book describes our sampling frame and design in more detail

## Impact Results

*Analysis Strategy*

The primary analysis of program impact was conducted within a hierarchical multiple regression framework. This framework was modified, depending on the type of sample being analyzed. For panel samples (reported here), the posttest scores on the variable of interest were used as the dependent variable and predictor variables were entered into the regression equation in three distinct groupings: (a) pretest scores; (b) important covariates; and (c) the treatment dummy variable. The following covariates were used for virtually all regression analyses because of their demonstrated importance in prior research: the respondent's sex, age, race, educational level, occupancy status (owner or renter), victimization history, and vicarious victimization history (knowledge of other victims). If the presence or absence of the crime prevention program could add significantly to the amount of variance in the posttest already explained by the pretest and other covariates, this was generally interpreted as evidence of a "treatment effect," that is, the program made a difference in the outcome variable of interest.

*Interpreting Tables* For all regression analyses, the tables contain information about changes in the proportion of variance accounted for at each step in the hierarchical procedure (See "Cum R2"), the standardized regression coefficient associated with the treatment variable (See "Beta") and the F value used to test the significance of that beta (See "F Beta"). For the panel analyses, similar information is also provided with regard to the role of the pretest. To avoid the presentation of massive tables, the betas and F values for the seven individual covariates are not shown.

Although the regression analyses used to test treatment effects adjusted posttest scores for pretest differences, the pretest adjustments are *not* included in the presentation of means so that reasonable comparisons can be made between the pretest (or Time 1 data) and post test.

*Testing the Main Hypotheses*

The results will be presented as they pertain to each of the seven main hypothesis guiding this impact evaluation. Thus, each hypothesis is stated below and then examined in light of the available data. The results reported here—which comprise the bulk of the findings—are based on neighborhood-level comparisons of treated and untreated areas using panel data. The independent-samples data are not reported here for several reasons. In addition to space considerations, we feel that the panel data provide a stronger test of hypotheses pertaining to change in individual behaviors and perceptions. We should also note that most of the independent-sample results were nonsignificant.

*Testing Hypothesis One: Increased Exposure and Participation*

The first hypothesis states that local community organizations, in their efforts to implement the program, should be able to (a) improve residents' awareness of local opportunities to participate in crime prevention activities and (b) stimulate actual participation in these events. These two outcomes are considered direct evidence of treatment implementation.

*Exposure/Awareness* The results suggest that organizations were quite successful at exposing local residents to the program, that is, making them aware of opportunities to get involved in crime prevention activities. As Table 6.1 shows, there were significant "treatment effects" in seven of the eight comparisons. That is, after controlling for pretest differences and other covariates, treated neighborhoods showed significant gains relative to untreated neighborhoods over a one year period in terms of having "heard or read about" and having had the "opportunity to attend" a "neighborhood crime prevention meeting" or "block watch program on your block."

The adjusted mean changes on the four-item exposure scale are shown in Table 6.2. All four treated neighborhoods showed increases in residents' exposure to the treatment from 1983 to 1984. However, two of the four—Northeast Austin Organization (NAO) and Edgewater Community Council (ECC)—may have capitalized on fairly large (and significant) pretest differences that were present between the treated and untreated areas.

A closer look at the items in the exposure scale revealed that most of the changes were attributable to changes in exposure to block watch meetings rather than neighborhood meetings. The unadjusted panel percentages indicate that the four treated areas showed an overall increase in *exposure to block watch* by 8 percent (from 21.1 percent to 29.2 percent of the residents), while comparison neighborhoods declined by 2.7 percent (from 11.6 percent to 8.9 percent) and the citywide remained unchanged, as 16.8 percent of Chicagoans claimed awareness of block watch meetings on their block in both 1983 and 1984. In contrast, a 5.7 percent rise in *exposure to neighborhood meetings* in treated areas was overshadowed by a 7.8 percent increase in the comparison areas and a 2.8 percent increase citywide.

*Participation* Actual levels of participation in relevant crime prevention

TABLE 6-1
Exposure to Crime Prevention Meetings

| Comparison | Predictors | Cum R² | F Change | BETA | F BETA |
|---|---|---|---|---|---|
| Northwest Neighborhood | Pretest | .69 | 69.69*** | .34 | 52.62*** |
| Federation vs. | Covariates[2] | .23 | 4.11*** | — | — |
| Comparison Neighborhoods | Treatment | .24 | 4.56* | .10 | 4.56* |
| Northwest Neighborhood | Pretest | .17 | 117.97*** | .40 | 108.14*** |
| Federation vs. | Covariates | .21 | 3.01** | — | — |
| Citywide Sample | Treatment | .22 | 6.68** | .12 | 6.68** |
| Northeast Austin | Pretest | .35 | 99.20*** | .48 | 52.17*** |
| Organization vs. | Covariates | .39 | 1.47 | — | — |
| Comparison Neighborhoods | Treatment | .40 | 3.23 | .12 | 3.23 |
| Northeast Austin | Pretest | .23 | 124.15*** | .42 | 86.55*** |
| Organization vs. | Covariates | .26 | 2.02* | — | — |
| Citywide Sample | Treatment | .27 | 8.60** | .14 | 8.60** |
| Back of Yards Neighbor- | Pretest | .23 | 51.55*** | .48 | 43.66*** |
| hood Council vs. | Covariates | .27 | .88 | — | — |
| Comparison Neighborhoods | Treatment | .29 | 5.34* | .16 | 5.34* |
| Back of Yards Neighbor- | Pretest | .17 | 80.24*** | .39 | 70.24*** |
| hood Council vs. | Covariates | .20 | 1.82 | — | — |
| Citywide Sample | Treatment | .21 | 4.21* | .10 | 4.21* |
| Edgewater Community | Pretest | .14 | 41.65*** | .30 | 24.83*** |
| Council vs. | Covariates | .18 | 1.40 | — | — |
| Comparison Neighborhoods | Treatment | .22 | 12.50*** | .21 | 12.50*** |
| Edgewater Community | Pretest | .18 | 104.60*** | .35 | 70.60*** |
| Council vs. | Covariates | .21 | 2.19* | — | — |
| Citywide Sample | Treatment | .25 | 23.82*** | .22 | 23.82*** |
| Auburn-Gresham | Pretest | .17 | 102.42*** | .37 | 78.25*** |
| vs. | Covariates | .23 | 3.66*** | — | — |
| Citywide Sample | Treatment | .23 | 4.92* | .12 | 4.92* |

[1]$p < .10$; *$p < .05$; **$p < .01$; ***$p < .001$
[2]Covariates = sex, age, race, education, home ownership, victimization experience, vicarious victimization (knowledge of victims).

meetings provide a second and more stringent test of Hypothesis One. It is one thing to make citizens aware of crime prevention meetings, but another to get them to attend and participate. While the effects on participation were not as strong as the effects on exposure (as would be expected), nevertheless, the panel data showed fairly consistent support for this hypothesis. As shown in Table 6.3, all four neighborhoods were able to distinguish themselves on participation levels from one of their two control groups, but none was able to distinguish itself from both control groups.

TABLE 6-2
Changes in Exposure to Crime Prevention Meetings
(Adjusted Means[1])

| Area | 1983 Pretest | 1984 Post test |
| --- | --- | --- |
| | TIME OF MEASUREMENT | |
| Citywide Sample | 1.00 | 1.15 |
| Northwest Neighborhood Federation | 1.01 | 1.45 |
| Comparison Neighborhoods | .92 | 1.14 |
| Northeast Austin Organization | 1.91 | 2.04 |
| Comparison Neighborhoods | 1.03 | 1.15 |
| Back of Yards Neighborhood Council | 1.01 | 1.53 |
| Comparison Neighborhoods | 1.19 | 1.01 |
| Edgewater Community Council | 1.70 | 2.16 |
| Comparison Neighborhoods | 1.16 | 1.30 |

[1]Adjusted for all covariates in the regression equation except the pretest.

Table 6.4 shows the direction of these changes over time. Indeed, all four treated neighborhoods demonstrated *increases* in participation levels among local residents relative to at least one control group. However, the Northeast Austin Organization was able to capitalize on *declining* participation in the untreated comparison neighborhoods. Only the Northwest Neighborhood Federation was able to demonstrate a significant increase relative to the Chicago citywide sample.

These participation findings should be tempered by our assessment of the amount and prevalence of participation and by extensive field work on the level of investment by each community organization. First, we should note that, although participation levels increased significantly relative to certain control groups, both the magnitude of change and the absolute levels of participation remain rather small. For example, the unadjusted panel percentages indicate that treated areas *as a whole* showed only a 3.9 percent increase in participation, from 12.3 percent of the residents in 1983 to 16.2 percent in 1984. The citywide control group showed an increase of 7.0 percent (from 6.1 percent to 13.1 percent of Chicagoans) and the neighborhood control groups showed a 1.4 percent rise in participation (from 8.1 percent to 9.5 percent).

Our field work clearly suggests that only one organization—the Northwest Neighborhood Federation—seriously adopted the block watch philosophy and program. Two groups—Northeast Austin and Back of the Yards—preferred to implement the program via neighborhood meetings

TABLE 6-3
Participation in Crime Prevention Meetings

| Comparison | Predictors | Cum R² | F Change | BETA | F BETA |
|---|---|---|---|---|---|
| Northwest Neighborhood | Pretest | .11 | 47.90*** | .34 | 41.10*** |
| Federation vs. | Covariates² | .15 | 1.78 | — | — |
| Comparison Neighborhoods | Treatment | .15 | 1.90 | .07 | 1.90 |
| Northwest Neighborhood | Pretest | .14 | 91.12*** | .37 | 87.04*** |
| Federation vs. | Covariates | .16 | 1.41 | — | — |
| Citywide Sample | Treatment | .17 | 6.97** | .12 | 6.97** |
| Northeast Austin | Pretest | .11 | 22.19*** | .28 | 19.02*** |
| Organization vs. | Covariates | .30 | 5.57*** | — | — |
| Comparison Neighborhoods | Treatment | .33 | 6.45** | .18 | 6.45** |
| Northeast Austin | Pretest | .20 | 108.41*** | .44 | 101.31*** |
| Organization vs. | Covariates | .23 | 1.64 | — | — |
| Citywide Sample | Treatment | .24 | 3.22 | .09 | 3.22¹ |
| Back of Yards Neighbor- | Pretest | .22 | 42.27*** | .46 | 43.49*** |
| hood Council vs. | Covariates | .25 | .73 | — | — |
| Comparison Neighborhoods | Treatment | .27 | 3.67 | .13 | 3.67¹ |
| Back of Yards Neighbor- | Pretest | .17 | 80.90*** | .41 | 77.98*** |
| hood Council vs. | Covariates | .19 | 1.16 | — | — |
| Citywide Sample | Treatment | .19 | 2.21 | .08 | 2.21 |
| Edgewater Community | Pretest | .11 | 29.67*** | .29 | 21.88*** |
| Council vs. | Covariates | .15 | 1.35 | — | — |
| Comparison Neighborhoods | Treatment | .16 | 4.31* | .13 | 4.31* |
| Edgewater Community | Pretest | .13 | 70.86*** | .34 | 59.27*** |
| Council vs. | Covariates | .16 | 1.85 | — | — |
| Citywide Sample | Treatment | .16 | 3.21 | .08 | 3.21 |
| Auburn-Gresham | Pretest | .20 | 119.94*** | .43 | 105.40*** |
| vs. | Covariates | .21 | 1.24 | — | — |
| Citywide Sample | Treatment | .21 | .01 | .01 | .01 |

¹p < .10; *p < .05; **p < .01; ***p < .01
²Covariates = sex, age, race, education, home ownership, victimization experience, vicarious victimization (knowledge of victims).

geared to the entire community or to specific audiences (e.g., church groups). Thus, holding a few neighborhood meetings over the course of the year might be sufficient to produce a significant increase in neighborhood participation (as measured by our surveys). Our field work indicates that the Edgewater Community Council started only one block watch as part of the program, but the group continued to meet on a regular basis. Thus, attendance at ECC meetings may have been sufficient to account for the increase in participation, but this is only speculation.

TABLE 6-4
Changes in Participation in Crime Prevention Meetings
(Adjusted Means[1])

| Area | TIME OF MEASUREMENT | |
|---|---|---|
| | 1983 Pretest | 1984 Post test |
| Citywide Sample | .08 | .13 |
| Northwest Neighborhood Federation | .10 | .24 |
| Comparison Neighborhoods | .06 | .15 |
| Northeast Austin Organization | .14 | .20 |
| Comparison Neighborhoods | .11 | .06 |
| Back of Yards Neighborhood Council | .05 | .19 |
| Comparison Neighborhoods | .07 | .09 |
| Edgewater Community Council | .17 | .24 |
| Comparison Neighborhoods | .14 | .09 |

[1]Adjusted for all covariates in the regression equation except the pretest.

In sum, we found some consistent, albeit, weak support for Hypothesis One. Residents in treated neighborhoods showed significant increases in awareness of, and participation in, crime prevention meetings relative to certain untreated areas. While these data stand as encouraging evidence that the organizations did, in fact, implement some type of program, there remain serious doubts about the strength/dosage of the treatment given the limited number of people involved, number of meetings held, and number of blocks organized during the implementation period.

*Testing Hypothesis Two: Greater Efficacy and Responsibility*

Hypothesis Two states that contact with the program, either in terms of greater awareness or actual participation, should enhance feelings of efficacy about local collective action and increase the tendency to attribute responsibility to citizens (rather than police) for the prevention of crime. First, we will summarize the results on three efficacy scales, and then look at perceived responsibility for crime prevention.

*Efficacy of Action* Did the intervention help to "empower" the local residents and make them feel that people on their block can make a difference in the neighborhood? The results in Table 6.5 indicate that feelings of efficacy about block level action unexpectedly *declined* in two neighborhoods (NNF and BYNC), while it *increased* in two others as predicted (NAO and ECC). The adjusted means are shown in Table 6.6. Although

TABLE 6-5
Perceived Efficacy of Block-Level Action

| Comparison | Predictors | Cum R² | F Change | BETA | F BETA |
|---|---|---|---|---|---|
| Northwest Neighborhood | Pretest | .06 | 20.79*** | .24 | 20.99*** |
| Federation vs. | Covariates[2] | .07 | .85 | — | — |
| Comparison Neighborhoods | Treatment | .10 | 7.72** | − .15 | 7.72** |
| Northwest Neighborhood | Pretest | .12 | 68.88*** | .31 | 56.75*** |
| . Federation vs. | Covariates | .14 | 1.67[1] | — | — |
| Citywide Sample | Treatment | .14 | .16 | − .02 | .16 |
| Northeast Austin | Pretest | .17 | 35.51*** | .43 | 34.55*** |
| Organization vs. | Covariates | .20 | .77 | — | — |
| Comparison Neighborhoods | Treatment | .20 | .73 | .07 | .73 |
| Northeast Austin | Pretest | .17 | 82.54*** | .39 | 69.20*** |
| Organization vs. | Covariates | .19 | 1.16 | — | — |
| Citywide Sample | Treatment | .20 | 3.21 | .09 | 3.21[1] |
| Back of Yards Neighbor- | Pretest | .09 | 15.75*** | .26 | 10.89*** |
| hood Council vs. | Covariates | .11 | .49 | — | — |
| Comparison Neighborhoods | Treatment | .14 | 5.07* | − .17 | 5.07* |
| Back of Yards Neighbor- | Pretest | .15 | 68.88*** | .35 | 54.12*** |
| hood Council vs. | Covariates | .18 | 1.70[1] | — | — |
| Citywide Sample | Treatment | .19 | .91 | − .05 | .91 |
| Edgewater Community | Pretest | .13 | 35.75*** | .35 | 33.40*** |
| Council vs. | Covariates | .16 | .89 | — | — |
| Comparison Neighborhoods | Treatment | .17 | 5.22* | .14 | 5.22* |
| Edgewater Community | Pretest | .14 | 75.68*** | .35 | 61.70*** |
| Council vs. | Covariates | .17 | 1.52 | — | — |
| Citywide Sample | Treatment | .17 | 3.78* | .09 | 3.78* |
| Auburn-Gresham | Pretest | .13 | 71.18*** | .32 | 51.70*** |
| vs. | Covariates | .17 | 2.21* | — | — |
| Citywide Sample | Treatment | .17 | .00 | .00 | .00 |

[1]p < .10; *p < .05; **p < .01; ***p < .001
[2]Covariates = sex, age, race, education, home ownership, victimization experience, vicarious
victimization (knowledge of victims).

NNF and BYNC showed declines in efficacy relative to comparison neighborhoods, they did not show more rapid declines than the city as a whole.

A second question is whether the programs changed residents' attitudes about the efficacy of collective crime prevention behavior, such as block watches and citizen patrols. The results indicate no effects across all comparisons. Thus, overall, residents' beliefs about the helpfulness of collective citizen action in preventing crime were not altered by these programs.

A third question is whether the interventions persuaded residents to

TABLE 6-6
Changes in Perceived Efficacy of Block-Level Actions
(Adjusted Means[1])

| Area | TIME OF MEASUREMENT | |
| --- | --- | --- |
| | 1983 Pretest | 1984 Post test |
| Citywide Sample | 1.72 | 1.63 |
| Northwest Neighborhood Federation | 1.59 | 1.50 |
| Comparison Neighborhoods | 1.66 | 1.67 |
| Northeast Austin Organization | 1.61 | 1.75 |
| Comparison Neighborhoods | 1.63 | 1.64 |
| Back of Yards Neighborhood Council | 1.54 | 1.47 |
| Comparison Neighborhoods | 1.63 | 1.70 |
| Edgewater Community Council | 1.65 | 1.69 |
| Comparison Neighborhoods | 1.71 | 1.50 |

[1]Adjusted for all covariates in the regression equation except the pretest.

believe more strongly in the efficacy of individual home protection measures, such as installing alarm systems or special locks. This was not the case. The results show a consistent absence of effects on the perceived efficacy of individual target hardening. Only BYNC showed a marginally significant effect, and the direction of change was counter to the hypothesis, i.e., decreased efficacy in comparison to the citywide sample.

*Responsibility for Action* Did the programs influence residents to think that preventing crime is more the responsibility of citizens than police? The results indicate that the treatments generally had no effect on attributions of responsibility for crime prevention. However, for the one neighborhood where significant effects were observed, the results again run counter to the hypothesis. Specifically, NAO residents attributed *less* responsibility to citizens and *more* responsibility to the police in comparison to changes in both control groups.

In sum, the support for Hypothesis Two regarding enhancement of efficacy and responsibility is weak, at best. With few exceptions, attributions of responsibility for crime prevention and the perceived efficacy of collective crime prevention were unaffected by the treatment. The third outcome measure—efficacy of block–level action—showed contradictory results, as some neighborhoods increased and others decreased. The declines in efficacy occurred in NNF (which used the block watch model) and BYNC (which encouraged residents to rely on BYNC to handle problems) while the increases occurred in NAO (which held neighborhood–wide meetings, as well as block club meetings, to respond to pressing issues) and ECC (whose strategy was never implemented). One might ask—how could NAO show *increases* in feelings of efficacy, but *decreases* in citizens' responsibility for preventing crime? This outcome is possible. One of the repeated messages of community organizers (and NAO in particular) is that citizens can make a difference by organizing themselves and pressuring the police to be accountable and responsive to the needs of their community. The decline in efficacy among those who lived in the NNF area may be attributable to the nature of the Block Watch meetings, as discussed later in this chapter.

*Hypothesis Three: Behavioral Changes*

Community crime prevention programs are expected to produce behavioral changes among citizens both in terms of efforts to prevent future victimization and efforts to regulate social behavior. In this section, we will summarize the results from five separate behavioral scales pertinent to this hypothesis, including measures of individual preventive actions, collective preventive actions, and willingness to intervene in neighborhood problems. Overall, the findings are not supportive of Hypothesis Three, and as such, provide little evidence that the interventions were successful at changing residents' behavior over a one–year period. The exceptions to this general conclusion are noted.

*Protective Behaviors* First, we hypothesized that programs would increase individual home protection behaviors, such as installing better locks, engraving valuable property, or having a home security survey. Two of the four neighborhoods (NNF and NAO) showed increases in home protection behavior relative to the citywide sample, but the NNF difference was only marginally significant. These increases did not differ from their comparison neighborhoods where increases were also occurring. Thus, only two of eight comparisons revealed changes in home protection behavior.

We also hypothesized that having more information about crime or having crime become a more salient issue might increase personal protective behaviors, such as watching out for suspicious persons or avoiding certain types of strangers. This was not true, as none of the panel sample comparisons showed any program effects.

*Victimization Reporting* Crime prevention programs typically encourage citizens to report crime to the police, especially their own experiences with victimization. We hypothesized that programs would produce an increase in the *percentage* of victimizations reported to the police. There was little consistent support for this hypothesis. The NAO neighborhood showed an increase in reporting relative to Chicago, while the ECC showed a marginally significant decrease.

*Collective Surveillance* Central to the block watch concept is the notion of "neighboring," whereby block residents take on a territorial interest in their immediate environment and collectively protect each other and their property from criminal intruders. In this context, we hypothesized that residents in the treated areas would show increases in the tendency to ask neighbors to watch their home while they were away. The results indicate almost no support for this hypothesis. Only NNF—the neighborhood which fully adopted the block watch model—was able to show an increase in requests for neighbors to watch their homes, and this change was only marginally significant.

*Taking Action Against Neighborhood Problems* Assuming that these programs encourage the exercise of informal social control and enhance citizen efficacy, we hypothesized that local residents, when faced with identifiable neighborhood problems, would be more inclined to intervene and take some form of action to help solve these problems. Looking at the percentage of big "problems" in the neighborhood for which residents took some action (ten–item scale), we found little support for this hypothesis. In fact, the one significant finding is in the opposite direction, showing a *decrease* in the tendency to take action among NAO residents relative to the comparison neighborhoods. This finding is consistent with the NAO message that taxpayers hire police officers to resolve neighborhood problems.

In sum, the total picture with regard to behavioral changes is not supportive of Hypothesis Three. The vast majority of comparisons were nonsignificant. However, some of the differences are noteworthy, perhaps indicating patterns *within* neighborhoods rather than *across* neighborhoods. For example, residents in the NAO target area are more likely to call on the police when victimized, but less likely to intervene themselves to resolve neighborhood incidents. NNF residents are somewhat more inclined to "watch out" for suspicious action and lock their doors as directed by the Block Watch Program.

*Hypothesis Four: Social Integration*

A central tenet of community crime prevention theorists is that collective activity has the capacity to enhance social integration among community residents, thus making the neighborhood a better social environment in which to live. Two measures of social integration were used to test Hypothesis Four—the self–reported frequency of spontaneous verbal interaction with neighbors on the street, and the proportion of block residents that they know by name. There was no support for the hypothesis that these programs would increase the frequency of informal "chatting" on the street among neighbors. In addition, residents in three out of four neighborhoods showed no evidence of an increase in the proportion of block residents they know by name. The one neighborhood that did change provides evidence against the hypothesis. Specifically, NAO showed a significant *reduction* in the proportion of residents known by name relative to both control groups.

*Hypothesis Five: Reduced Crime and Incivility*

Assuming that all the mechanisms and processes posited in earlier hypotheses are in place, two major outcomes that should be expected are: (a) a reduction in criminal victimization and (b) a reduction in various types of incivility or disorder. To test this hypothesis, we examined the impact of the programs on five different scales—two measuring victimization and three measuring different forms of disorder.

*Victimization Experience* The results revealed an interesting mixture of changes in victimization experience. Three of the four neighborhoods showed significant changes in the average number of victimizations per respondent, but two of these three run counter to the hypothesis. As suggested by the betas in Table 6.7 and confirmed by an inspection of the means, NAO and BYNC showed significant *increases* in the number of victimizations per respondent between 1983 and 1984. In contrast, NNF showed a marginally significant *decrease* in victimization experiences. Victimization levels in Chicago remained very stable between 1983 and 1984.

*Vicarious Victimization* Indirect or vicarious victimization was measured by asking respondents if they "personally know anyone" (other than themselves) who has been a victim of serious crime in the past year (respondents were asked about a cluster of personal and property crimes in two items). Paralleling the victimization results, the findings revealed *increases* in the number of vicarious victimizations in NAO. While the betas also suggested a marginally significant differential change in NNF and BYNC in an unfavorable direction, an inspection of the means revealed that vicarious victimization was actually decreasing in these areas, but just not as rapidly as the comparison neighborhoods. In sum, there is no support for the hypothesis that programs will yield reductions in vicarious victimization, and some evidence to the contrary.

*Youth Disorder* The amount of youth disorder in these neighborhoods (e.g. "hanging out," graffiti, drugs, gangs) was expected to decline as another indicator of program success. There were only two changes and they went in opposite directions. Contrary to the hypothesis, youth disorder

TABLE 6-7
Victimization Experience
(Eleven-item scale including personal and property crimes)

| Comparison | Predictors | Cum $R^2$ | F Change | BETA | F BETA |
|---|---|---|---|---|---|
| Northwest Neighborhood | Pretest | .17 | 78.15*** | .43 | 79.20*** |
| Federation vs. | Covariates[2] | .20 | 1.49 | — | — |
| Comparison Neighborhoods | Treatment | .20 | .30 | .03 | .30 |
| Northwest Neighborhood | Pretest | .26 | 192.72*** | .50 | 181.62*** |
| Federation vs. | Covariates | .27 | .90 | — | — |
| Citywide Sample | Treatment | .27 | 3.17 | −.08 | 3.17[1] |
| Northeast Austin | Pretest | .22 | 56.66*** | .47 | 50.25*** |
| Organization vs. | Covariates | .25 | .94 | — | — |
| Comparison Neighborhoods | Treatment | .28 | 8.83** | .21 | 8.83** |
| Northeast Austin | Pretest | .30 | 180.27*** | .53 | 167.78*** |
| Organization vs. | Covariates | .31 | .61 | — | — |
| Citywide Sample | Treatment | .31 | 4.97* | .10 | 4.97* |
| Back of Yards Neighbor- | Pretest | .20 | 42.09*** | .42 | 31.72*** |
| hood Council vs. | Covariates | .23 | .85 | — | — |
| Comparison Neighborhoods | Treatment | .24 | 2.45 | .11 | 2.45 |
| Back of Yards Neighbor- | Pretest | .31 | 179.39*** | .53 | 156.39*** |
| hood Council vs. | Covariates | .31 | .39 | — | — |
| Citywide Sample | Treatment | .32 | 4.28* | .10 | 4.28* |
| Edgewater Community | Pretest | .19 | 59.08*** | .43 | 57.84*** |
| Council vs. | Covariates | .24 | 2.18* | — | — |
| Comparison Neighborhoods | Treatment | .25 | .74 | −.05 | .74 |
| Edgewater Community | Pretest | .29 | 195.56*** | .53 | 182.20*** |
| Council vs. | Covariates | .30 | 1.13 | — | — |
| Citywide Sample | Treatment | .30 | .20 | −.02 | .20 |
| Auburn-Gresham | Pretest | .30 | 209.97*** | .52 | 184.88*** |
| vs. | Covariates | .32 | 1.57 | — | — |
| Citywide Sample | Treatment | .32 | .75 | −.04 | .75 |

[1]p < .10; *p < .05; **p < .01; ***p < .001
[2]Covariates = sex, age, race, education, home ownership, victimization experience, vicarious victimization (knowledge of victims).

increased in NAO relative to comparison neighborhoods. Only ECC showed a decline in youth disorder as predicted, but the change was only marginally significant.

*Youth Rejection of Social Control* Another measure of disorder which more directly examines the success of social control efforts is the extent to which neighborhood youths are viewed as respectful of property and people, law abiding, and responsive to parental requests. Consistent with the hypothesis, two neighborhoods (NNF and BYNC) showed significant reductions in the perceived amount of youth rejection of social control.

*Neighborhood Deterioration* In addition to addressing social disorder, community crime prevention programs oftentimes seek to improve the physical environment because of the close connection between neighborhood deterioration and crime. Using a three–item neighborhood deterioration scale (covering abandoned buildings or vehicles, garbage or litter, and disinterested landlords), we sought to measure residents' perceptions of the physical environment in a way that might detect disinvestment in the community. The results indicate that only one neighborhood—NNF—was able to show any perceived improvement in the physical environment and this change was in relationship to the citywide sample.

In sum, we found no consistent support for Hypothesis Five regarding reductions in crime, social disorder, and "physical" disorder. In fact, the significant changes were generally in the direction of *increases* rather than decreases in these problem areas. Specifically, there were more increases than decreases in both direct and vicarious victimization levels, as well as in youth disorder. Scales measuring youth rejection of social control and neighborhood deterioration were generally unchanged, but NNF was able to show some consistent support for the hypothesis across each of these scales.

*Hypothesis Six: Reduced Fear and Perceived Crime Rates*

According to Hypothesis Six, one of the major outcomes of community crime prevention programs should be a reduction in residents' fear of crime and a drop in the amount of crime they perceive in their neighborhood. Although fear of crime and perceptions of the crime problem are conceptually and empirically distinct constructs (See Baumer & Rosenbaum, 1981), for simplicity of presentation, we will discuss them together under a general hypothesis about psychological responses. Three scales were employed: fear of personal crime, fear of property crime, and perceptions of neighborhood crime.

*Fear of Personal Crime* This fear scale measures individual concern about being harmed or threatened while walking alone in one's own neighborhood. Contrary to the hypothesis, the results indicated significant *increases* in fear of personal crime in three of the four neighborhoods. Table 6.8 shows that for NNF, these changes occurred in relationship to comparison neighborhoods but not in relationship to the city as a whole. For BYNC and NAO, however, the increase in fear of personal crime was observed relative to both control groups. The adjusted means are shown in Table 6.9.

TABLE 6-8
Fear of Personal Crime

| Comparison | Predictors | Cum R² | F Change | BETA | F BETA |
|---|---|---|---|---|---|
| Northwest Neighborhood | Pretest | .48 | 338.90*** | .54 | 160.79*** |
| Federation vs. | Covariates² | .54 | 5.81*** | — | — |
| Comparison Neighborhoods | Treatment | .55 | 6.48** | .09 | 6.48** |
| Northwest Neighborhood | Pretest | .45 | 459.01*** | .59 | 279.32*** |
| Federation vs. | Covariates | .48 | 3.82*** | — | — |
| Citywide Sample | Treatment | .48 | .08 | .01 | .08 |
| Northeast Austin | Pretest | .44 | 147.07*** | .45 | 55.42*** |
| Organization vs. | Covariates | .53 | 4.01*** | — | — |
| Comparison Neighborhoods | Treatment | .55 | 6.48** | .15 | 6.84** |
| Northeast Austin | Pretest | .41 | 296.92*** | .56 | 181.24*** |
| Organization vs. | Covariates | .45 | 2.83** | — | — |
| Citywide Sample | Treatment | .45 | 3.59¹ | .08 | 3.59¹ |
| Back of Yards Neighbor- | Pretest | .38 | 101.25*** | .52 | 63.86*** |
| hood Council vs. | Covariates | .44 | 1.98* | — | — |
| Comparison Neighborhoods | Treatment | .49 | 15.92*** | .24 | 15.92*** |
| Back of Yards Neighbor- | Pretest | .41 | 277.61*** | .58 | 187.45*** |
| hood Council vs. | Covariates | .44 | 2.43** | — | — |
| Citywide Sample | Treatment | .46 | 12.79*** | .15 | 12.79** |
| Edgewater Community | Pretest | .47 | 226.80*** | .53 | 97.15*** |
| Council vs. | Covariates | .54 | 4.09*** | — | — |
| Comparison Neighborhoods | Treatment | .54 | .42 | − .03 | .42 |
| Edgewater Community | Pretest | .45 | 393.77*** | .59 | 221.71*** |
| Council vs. | Covariates | .48 | 2.59** | — | — |
| Citywide Sample | Treatment | .48 | .08 | − .01 | .08 |
| Auburn-Gresham | Pretest | .45 | 398.61*** | .60 | 244.93*** |
| vs. | Covariates | .48 | 2.63** | — | — |
| Citywide Sample | Treatment | .48 | .17 | .02 | .17 |

¹p < .10; *p < .05; **p < .01; ***p < .001
²Covariates = sex, age, race, education, home ownership, victimization experience, vicarious victimization (knowledge of victims).

*Fear of Property Crime* This scale measures residents' fear of being victimized by property crime, primarily their concern about residential burglary. The results do not support the hypothesis. There are many nonsignificant findings, and the one significant result is in the opposite direction, showing an *increase* in fear of property crime. That is, fear of property crime increased in BYNC relative to its comparison neighborhoods.

*Perceptions of Neighborhood Crime* A four–item scale measured residents' perceptions of the *amount* of crime in their neighborhood. Contrary

TABLE 6-9
Fear of Personal Crime
(Adjusted Means[1])

|  | TIME OF MEASUREMENT | |
| Area | 1983 Pretest | 1984 Post test |
| --- | --- | --- |
| Citywide Sample | 2.32 | 2.37 |
| Northwest Neighborhood Federation | 2.14 | 2.23 |
| Comparison Neighborhoods | 1.85 | 1.89 |
| Northeast Austin Organization | 2.43 | 2.52 |
| Comparison Neighborhoods | 2.10 | 2.07 |
| Back of Yards Neighborhood Council | 2.41 | 2.81 |
| Comparison Neighborhoods | 2.38 | 2.07 |
| Edgewater Community Council | 2.25 | 2.57 |
| Comparison Neighborhoods | 2.05 | 2.59 |

[1]Adjusted for all covariates in the regression equation except the pretest.

to the hypothesis, the results indicate that residents in two of the four treated neighborhoods experienced *increases* in the amount of crime in their immediate environments. NNF residents perceived more neighborhood crime relative to residents in comparison areas, but not relative to the citywide sample. NAO residents felt a considerable rise in local crime rates relative to both control groups.

In sum, the available evidence from three outcome measures not only failed to support Hypothesis Six, but showed unexpected changes in the opposite direction. Specifically, there were some consistent findings which indicate *increases* in fear of personal crime and *increases* in perceptions of local crime rates.

*Hypothesis Seven: Increased Optimism and Attachment to Neighborhood*

Hypothesis Seven addresses the final outcome of these interventions. If all goes well, the programs should improve residents' optimism about the future of their neighborhood and increase their attachment to the area as a place of live. Two scales were used to test this hypothesis—a two–item scale measuring residents' optimism about neighborhood change in the past year and in the two years ahead (i.e. whether the neighborhood is getting "better" "worse" or "staying about the same"), and a single–item scale asking residents about their likelihood of moving in the next two years.

Contrary to the hypothesis, the results showed significant *declines* in

TABLE 6-10
Optimism About Neighborhood Change

| Comparison | Predictors | Cum R² | F Change | BETA | F BETA |
|---|---|---|---|---|---|
| Northwest Neighborhood | Pretest | .16 | 68.74*** | .36 | 54.69*** |
| Federation vs. | Covariates² | .20 | 2.51** | — | — |
| Comparison Neighborhoods | Treatment | .21 | 5.10* | − .11 | 5.10* |
| Northwest Neighborhood | Pretest | .16 | 104.37*** | .36 | 79.21*** |
| Federation vs. | Covariates | .19 | 2.18* | — | — |
| Citywide Sample | Treatment | .19 | .40 | .03 | .40 |
| Northeast Austin | Pretest | .44 | 146.47*** | .58 | 81.51*** |
| Organization vs. | Covariates | .45 | .33 | — | — |
| Comparison Neighborhoods | Treatment | .48 | 11.41*** | − .23 | 11.41*** |
| Northeast Austin | Pretest | .25 | 141.25*** | .39 | 76.73*** |
| Organization vs. | Covariates | .28 | 2.05* | — | — |
| Citywide Sample | Treatment | .32 | 22.38*** | − .22 | 22.38*** |
| Back of Yards Neighbor- | Pretest | .33 | 82.73*** | .46 | 40.33*** |
| hood Council vs. | Covariates | .37 | 1.08 | — | — |
| Comparison Neighborhoods | Treatment | .43 | 16.35*** | − .29 | 16.35*** |
| Back of Yards Neighbor- | Pretest | .20 | 100.96*** | .37 | 60.31*** |
| hood Council vs. | Covariates | .24 | 2.41** | — | — |
| Citywide Sample | Treatment | .26 | 7.60** | − .14 | 7.60** |
| Edgewater Community | Pretest | .41 | 171.71*** | .62 | 142.98*** |
| Council vs. | Covariates | .43 | 1.03 | — | — |
| Comparison Neighborhoods | Treatment | .43 | 1.60 | .06 | 1.60 |
| Edgewater Community | Pretest | .20 | 123.11*** | .41 | 96.19*** |
| Council vs. | Covariates | .24 | 2.59** | — | — |
| Citywide Sample | Treatment | .25 | 4.02* | .09 | 4.02* |
| Auburn-Gresham | Pretest | .13 | 73.76*** | .34 | 63.62*** |
| vs. | Covariates | .16 | 2.14* | — | — |
| Citywide Sample | Treatment | .17 | .80 | .05 | .80 |

¹p < .10; *p < .05; **p < .01; ***p < .001
²Covariates = sex, age, race, education, home ownership, victimization experience, vicarious victimization (knowledge of victims).

residents' optimism about neighborhood change in three of the four neighborhoods (See Table 6.10). In other words, residents were more inclined after one year to report that their neighborhood is getting "worse" rather than "better." Although the control groups also showed declines in optimism, the treatment areas were declining at a faster rate. The fourth neighborhood—ECC—showed a significant increase in optimism about the neighborhood.

The changes in optimism are complicated by pretest differences in two of the neighborhoods. That is, NAO and BYNC residents were significantly less optimistic about the future of their neighborhoods than residents in the respective control groups prior to program implementation. Hence, there is a greater possibility of selection differences interacting with other factors (including the treatment) to produce these effects.

Changes in the likelihood of moving out of the neighborhood also ran counter to the hypothesis. Residents from two of the four neighborhoods (NAO and BYNC) revealed significant increases in their likelihood of moving relative to both control groups.

In sum, the available evidence goes against Hypothesis Seven. Three of the four neighborhoods showed *decreases* in optimism about changes in the neighborhood, and two of the four neighborhoods showed a *greater* likelihood of moving among residents.

## Summary and Conclusions

Several observations about these findings deserve mention. First, most of the analytic comparisons between the treated and untreated areas revealed no differential change over time. This indicates a failure to support most of the central hypotheses. Second, patterns of significant change were apparent across neighborhoods, with some neighborhoods showing very little change and others showing change on a number of dimensions. The two neighborhoods where "programs," per se, were not implemented to any significant degree (i.e., Auburn–Gresham and Edgewater Community Council) showed very few changes relative to control groups. In contrast, the remaining three neighborhoods showed substantially more changes.

A third observation is that there appear to be some interesting differences in the *pattern* of changes across neighborhoods, especially when we look at the two neighborhoods that made an effort to implement a program—Northwest Neighborhood Federation (NNF) and Northeast Austin Organization (NAO). Given their local interest in holding the police accountable, some of the observed changes in NAO would appear consistent with the group's goals. The observed changes indicate that NAO residents became more likely to call the police to report victimization, more likely to hold the police (*rather than* the citizens) responsible for preventing crime, and *less* likely to intervene themselves in neighborhood problems. Moreover, NAO residents reported feeling (somewhat) more efficacious at the block level in bringing about change. Perhaps these feelings are due to a belief that block residents can be instrumental in stimulating a police response if enough pressure is applied. However, NAO residents did not truly believe everything they were saying, *or* they have yet to see the benefits of these instrumental actions because there was widespread agreement among residents (on a number of dimensions) that their neighborhood had *gotten worse* during the time of the program. Specifically, during the time of program implementation, the problems of victimization, vicarious victimization, disorder, and fear of crime all increased, as well as residents' desire to move out of the neighborhood.

The area organized by the Northwest Neighborhood Federation did not show this same pattern of outcomes. The crime–related outcomes were somewhat more favorable and indicate a marginally significant reduction in victimization and improvement in the level of disorder. The NNF neighborhood is the only target area where a significant number of block watches were organized during the time of the evaluation. However, the price of community organizing may have been an increase in fear of crime and related perceptions. We should note that in the NNF area, perceptions and reality were not synchronized—the victimization/disorder changes were moving in one direction, while the fear/perception changes were headed in the opposite direction. In NAO, both perceptions and reality pointed in the same direction toward a worsening situation.

The issue of fear of crime deserves special attention because it has been placed in such a central position in the field of community crime prevention by practitioners and theoreticians alike. Fear reduction has become a primary goal of virtually all community crime prevention programs. Three of the four neighborhoods studied here experienced significant *increases* in fear of crime. Although the evidence is inconclusive, there is the possibility that these changes in perceptions were due to organizing efforts at the neighborhood and block levels. This possibility has motivated us to explore in greater detail the effects of small group meetings on group participants.

Finally, looking at the results in their entirety, the reader is reminded that (a) the large majority of findings showed "no difference" between neighborhoods that received the program and those that did not; and (b) the majority of significant findings ran *counter to* the main hypotheses. Whether these observations are indicative of theory failure, implementation failure, or measurement problems is an issue that we have debated elsewhere (see Rosenbaum, Lewis, and Grant, 1986).

# 7

# The Block Watch Experience

As far as the staff and leadership of CIS were concerned, block watch was the linchpin of their community crime prevention efforts. Arthur Sims noted, "CIS's judgment was that block watch was our bread–and–butter program, that Ford was interested enough in part because block watch had the track record, block watch had the evaluations that seemed to show that it was, on a policy level, generalizable." Sims felt that block watch had the potential to "build strong neighborhoods." He said, "To the best of my ability, I've tried to emphasize the block watch program which is, on evidence, best for the people in the neighorhoods." He explained that under LEAA funding, five of the ten community organizations chose block watch as their crime prevention strategy. When the LEAA funding ended, "I pushed [block watch] at the juncture on the grounds that I [already] described, and groups chose to stay with it and ECC (Edgewater Community Council) added it."

If there was some consensus to emphasize block watch (and this is not entirely certain, given discussions at Steering Committee meetings where group representatives complained that block watch was receiving attention to the exclusion of other crime prevention approaches), it was also evident from our field observations that the differing ideologies and structures of the groups in the program created different propensities for successfully implementing a block watch program. These differences and their effects on block watch organizing have been discussed. Nonetheless, if block watch is the "coin of the realm" in community crime prevention, then what actually happened at the block watch meetings (and whether the meetings took place at all) was significant for the effects the program had or did not have. Presumably, what took place at these meetings should help to explain the existence (or absence) of the hypothesized outcomes of this intervention, such as decreased fear of crime, increased feelings of social interaction, and increased optimism about the neighborhood.

The crime prevention field has been plagued by the twin problems of weak outcomes and poor descriptions of interventions. To put it simply, not much makes a difference and when it does, we don't know how the effects were achieved. Yin argues that too little attention has been paid to what the intervention is in crime prevention. What precisely are people doing when they say they are doing crime prevention? What behavior are they engaged in? Whom do they see? What do they do? Without examining these activities, we cannot interpret what we find about outcomes, no matter how successful. Without a good sense of what transpired in the name of the project, we cannot grasp the core of the activity being evaluated.

To explore the question of what the intervention was, we need to begin with observations of what happened at block watch meetings. To understand what the program accomplished and why, we have to start with what those who were involved did. This requires us to examine the interactions between organizers and the citizens of the targeted areas at block watch meetings. From this evaluative stance, we can begin to make sense of those activities and how they affected the participants themselves and the community at large.

Each of the groups in the program engaged in myriad activities, some of which were directly linked to crime prevention and some not. Each of these activities established its presence in the community and each, we may assume, had some effects on local residents, including their perceptions, feelings, and behaviors. If we are trying to measure the impact of block watch per se in these neighborhoods, however, then we have to focus more precisely on what happened at the block watch meetings and the internal and external activities which were spawned.

Each of the groups interpreted what crime prevention meant and what block watch meant in light of its own ideology and structure. In that sense, we are interpreting the behavior of five different groups and trying to account for systematic differences in our survey outcomes. Overall, however, we are concerned with whether there were behaviors and activities that grew out of the crime prevention programs in general and block watch efforts in particular that in some way could be reasonably correlated with the expected and hoped for outcomes of a community crime prevention program.

### Block Watch Meetings: What Happened?

Of all the groups, the Northwest Neighborhood Federation undertook the strongest and most concerted attempt to implement a block watch program during the period of our observations. This involved the establishment of 107 new block watches in a previously "untreated" area. Although this was half the number of block watches the Federation originally intended to establish, it still constituted a painstaking effort by staff and organization members. The Federation followed a fairly regularized format in establishing these watches. It began with an area organizer canvassing a block to let residents know about the block watch program, and finding a resident willing to host the first watch meeting on that block. This was not an easy task, as evidenced by the problems that both the Northeast Austin Organization and the Back of the Yards Neighborhood Council had in finding people willing to open up their homes to other area residents. Once the organizer found a host for the first meeting, he or she would then let all the other residents on the block know about the meeting through leaflets, door–to–door canvassing, and phone calls. At the first meeting of a block, usually held in the early evening or a weekend afternoon, the turnout was generally in the range of ten to twenty people. Residents were given the opportunity to meet each other, to express their concerns about the neighborhood, and then to hear the organizer discuss what the Federation was, what it had accomplished to solve other neighborhood problems, and what the block watch program was about. This also meant that the organizer would describe the nature of the crime problem in their neighborhood and why the block watch was an effective tool in dealing with it. The organizer would cite the Federation's success with block watch on other blocks in the neighborhood and why, through their collective efforts, they could do something to help themselves. Individuals were encouraged to express their feelings and also to begin thinking about a "social" response to what seemed to be their individual anxiety. The following excerpt from a block watch meeting in the Northwest Neighborhood Federation captures some of the flavor of what transpired at these meetings.

> The organizer began the meeting by giving some background on the Federation and how it got involved in a crime prevention program. She said the focus of the program was for people on a block to know one another better and to be alert to suspicious activity. If there are more people watching, there is a greater chance of detecting criminal activity. In addition, a person who saw some suspicious activity could then call a neighbor to alert him to it as well as calling the police. The neighbor would also in turn call the police and another neighbor.

> The organizer asked people to turn to the gold sheet in the packet of materials she had handed out to each one. This sheet was called "Are You A Burglar's Friend?" and was subtitled, "A do–it–yourself, step–by–step, item–by–item security check of your home." It focused on things like lighting, windows, doors, valuables, etc. A discussion was generated about whether it was useful to have more locks on your door. One of the hosts of the meeting contended that no lock could keep someone out who wanted to get in. The organizer said that could be true, but locks might make it too time consum-

ing for someone to try and get in. She gave the example of her own apartment where she lives alone and discussed the things she has done to make it safer. She said it was a question of deciding how much you wanted to invest to make your home safer.

The organizer mentioned the use of engraving pens and why they are important. She brought out a pen and said that any of them could use it if they wanted to. Someone asked if they would have to rent it from NNF and the organizer repeated that NNF lends them out for free. She said that items that are engraved with the owner's driver's license number were much easier to reclaim, whether they were found in a pawn shop or were being sold on the street.

A man in his late forties told of an example where he had recently called the police because it was obvious to him that someone had tried to break into his garage. He was proud of the fact that they couldn't get in, but said that although the policeman, who arrived about one hour after he called, noted it down as an "attempted burglary," he later heard over the police dispatch radio (which he seemed to be able to hear in his own home) that the case was reported in as "damage to property." The man felt that that was an inaccurate description of what had happened. The organizer pointed out that in the case of crime "ignorance is not bliss" and it would have been helpful in this case if he could have alerted his neighbors to the problem. Another man in his late forties responded to the story by noting that "there are a lot of stupid officers on the street."

The organizer then discussed the household inventory list in the packet and how this could let them know what was taken in the event of a burglary. There was some discussion about the best place to hide the list, since one wouldn't want a would–be robber to find it. She also discussed the "Hot Line" card which gave numbers to call. She made the point that they should not call their district office, but call 911 in an emergency since all the police cars are dispatched from downtown. When they called 911, the operator would have their address and name printed on a screen automatically, but that they could request that the officer who was responding to their call not have the name and address of the person making the complaint. It took a little while for people to understand what the organizer was saying, but the discussion of this topic did end after a few minutes.

At this point, one woman said she was unhappy because there was no street sign near her house. She said a friend had visited who got off the bus and couldn't figure out where her street was. Another participant said there was a street sign but that it was too high to be seen. He said it was high so that kids couldn't take it down. The organizer said this was an instance where they could work together to get something done, either by writing a petition or by all of them making the appropriate calls to the city. She emphasized that if just one person called it could be dismissed, but, if several people called, the city would have to take account of it. Another person complained about people who sped through the alleys. He said it was funny that many of them had kids who could be hurt by people doing that. One complained that all the streets had been made one way without anyone consulting them.

The host of the meeting commented that it was good to meet people on the block, that she really didn't know any of these people before although she herself was a long-time resident of the block.

At the end of the meeting, residents were asked to sign a phone tree and a volunteer was sought to represent the block on the local Anti-Crime Committee. A second meeting would be held, usually within two to four weeks, to both solidify the watch and to involve residents who did not attend the first meeting. The turnout at the second meeting was again in the range of ten to twenty people, some of whom had been present at the first meeting. One of the things the Federation attempted to accomplish at these meetings was to get people to confront their fears about crime and "residential transition" and to see that they, in conjunction with the Federation, could do something about these problems. Together, they could exert "control" over what was happening in their neighborhood and provide direction to future neighborhood development. To begin that process, residents were asked to join the phone tree through which they would call their neighbor and the police in the event of suspicious activity, to attend the local Anti-Crime Committee meetings, and to become active in other Federation projects. (The purpose of the phone tree was to have residents call the police and then alert their neighbors to suspicious activity and ask their neighbors to call the police, as well. This phone "blitz" was designed to speed police response. Residents were urged not to intervene in the criminal activity themselves. For those who did not become more active, the intervention largely was the block meeting itself and whatever correspondence they then received from the Federation. For those who did become more active, the Federation offered a number of participatory outlets. For the Federation, the block meetings provided a source of new recruits to pursue Federation goals related to crime and other neighborhood issues.

Could the block watch program be expected to accomplish many of its hypothesized outcomes, even when it was implemented as systematically and diligently as the Federation did? The basic intervention involved people talking to each other and perhaps seeing their world in a somewhat different way. It also involved for some a minimum of activities after the meeting itself, such as interacting occasionally with the Federation. For others, the commitment was greater, including participation in local and Federation Anti-Crime Committee activities. And for some others, they became more fully involved in Federation activities aimed at affecting local criminal justice and municipal institutions.

Rosenbaum (1987) questions why the block watch should be expected to produce all the things we hope for it. He notes that given the actual operation of the block watch, effects opposite to those predicted might also result. For instance, it is not inconceivable that when a group of individuals get together and talk about local crime problems, their fear of crime might increase as well as decrease. Fear of personal crime did increase over the year that the Federation operated its program. (It should be noted, however, that in neighborhoods like Back of the Yards, where people heard presentations about crime, but were not given the direct opportunity to form block watches, the increase in the fear of crime over the year was even more pronounced than for the Federation.) Moreover, what other behavioral changes resulted from these meetings? Certainly people were asked to increase their surveillance, and there is evidence that this did occur in the Federation area as both home protection behaviors and asking neighbors to watch their homes increased over the year. Rosenbaum (1987) points out, however, that such meetings gave residents little ability to "control" the behaviors of those who did not participate in the meetings, whether they were "good" or "bad" influences in the neighborhood. How could such an intervention be reasonably expected to affect crime rates? It should be noted that residents in The Northwest Neighborhood area did report decreased victimization experiences over the course of the year. Still, the extent to which crime rates were actually affected is uncertain. Finally, it is questionable whether a meeting of ten or twenty individuals once or twice throughout the year could greatly increase social interaction, feelings of efficacy, and optimism about the neighborhood in a densely populated urban setting. Although Northwest–side residents did report a decline in neighborhood deterioration over the year, their perceptions of neighborhood crime and their fear of personal crime increased, while their belief in the efficacy of block action and their optimism about the neighborhood decreased. As Rosenbaum (1987) notes, the question of what is the appropriate "dosage" and how such behaviors can be expected to increase "informal social control" has not been sufficiently researched. Nonetheless, through their crime prevention program, the Federation clearly was able to increase their "presence" and recognizability within their neighborhood, as well as increase their presence and their political demands on municipal institutions, including the local police department, the mayor's office, and the "unscrupulous" real estate agents in their neighborhood. This was clearly a neighborhood trying to fight the fear of residential transition, and though most of the predicted positive outcomes for the program did not materialize, the fact that residents of the neighborhood experienced fewer of the negative outcomes found for the Northeast Austin Organization and the Back of the Yards Neighborhood Council may be some small measure of the program's actual success.

The block watch programs of the Northeast Austin Organization and the Back of the Yards Neighborhood Council were neither as extensive nor as systematically implemented as the Federation's program. In addition, both areas were "neighborhoods in transition" where extensive demographic and economic changes were underway. The extent to which either of these factors accounts for the fewer positive outcomes and more negative outcomes on our survey in these two neighborhoods as compared to the Federation area is not clear. For NAO, crime was a salient issue to which considerable organizational resources were devoted. Nonetheless, this was a resource-poor organization with limited staff and time to devote to crime prevention. NAO clearly made its presence felt in the neighborhood through its various crime-related activities, such as the CB Patrol, community-wide meetings, and block club organizing. NAO organized twenty-three blocks into eight block clubs during the period of our observations. This involved getting residents within a two to three block area to meet, to discuss neighborhood problems, and to consider options for crime prevention. However, the block watch, the phone tree, and the surveillance goals appeared less important to this organization than its "sociability" goals and desires for improved responsiveness from criminal justice and municipal institutions. The following excerpt provides a glimpse of block watch meetings as they occurred in the Northeast Austin area.

> The meeting was chaired by a young black man. He said he thought it was important for everyone to participate on their blocks and in this club. He said, "We must help each other out." He spoke about the need to form a clean-up committee and get the young kids in the neighborhood involved. He said it was important for there to be representatives from each block at these meetings.
>
> At this point, a police officer entered the room. Midge interrupted the chair and said that she had asked the local commander to send someone from the Tac Squad to come to speak with them because people at the last meeting had several questions they wanted to ask them. The officer's name was Frank March. He said he was a "beat man," not a tac man, and had no idea why he was sent to this meeting. The commander told him to come and he thought he was responding to a complaint of a disturbance at this address.
>
> The officer was taciturn. One of the older white women said, "It's good to see you. It's nice to know how you look." March's face remained expressionless. He then said something about, "The way this district operates, you don't get assigned to the same beat." Midge asked him some questions about the number of cars assigned to each "sector" and he explained how it was organized. Throughout the whole time he was "on the spot," March fingered his gunbelt nervously. There were some questions about calling 911 and whether it was true that your name and address and phone number were flashed on a screen for the dispatcher to see. March said it was true, but that it is important for people to get involved. Midge added that it is helpful to the caller, if he is in some trouble, to have his address flashed on the screen. March then left the meeting.

Midge resumed by saying that it is important for people to watch the alleys between houses and to let their neighbors know when they are going on vacation. A young white man gave them some tips about securing their garages with a steel bolt. Midge mentioned that the Laurel Avenue Block Club would be meeting on Friday evening and they were the people who could coordinate the alley watch with the people on Long. Some of those present expressed interest in attending that Block Club meeting.

Midge also said that when people go out in their yards to work, they should lock up their houses. Midge said that about thirty families had already signed up on the phone tree and that that night a few more families would be added. She said that perhaps they could get the phone tree working before the next meeting. The chair suggested that people go out on their block and tell people about the club. Then he said that two reps from each block should meet before the next meeting to decide what they would talk about. Midge said the next meeting would be held on the third Wednesday in June. The chair said they should flyer the block, then contact people about the next meeting. Midge said these ideas were very good.

Our survey did reveal that Northeast Austin area residents in the target area were aware of the block watch program, were participating in it, were undertaking increased home protection behaviors, were reporting more victimizations to the police, and were likely to believe in the efficacy of block action. On the other hand, residents in the target area reported knowing fewer of their fellow block residents by name, an increase in youth disorder and victimization experiences, an increase in the fear of personal crime, a decreased optimism about their neighborhood and an increased likelihood of moving.

Here again, Rosenbaum's questions are relevant. How do we know that when we get people together to talk about crime, their fear of crime will not increase? How can a few meetings a year increase "social control," particularly when participants cannot control the behavior of those who do not attend the meetings? Finally, in urban areas that are experiencing fear and anxiety about the unknown and about change, are infrequent block meetings, community–wide forums, and a CB patrol sufficient to shape the social and economic future of a neighborhood? Clearly, NAO saw its mission as winning the hearts and minds of residents, convincing both older and newer residents to stay and fight and preserve what they had and to create political pressure to secure what they were losing. Clearly our survey revealed that their efforts had borne some fruit. Still, the goals of cooperation and stabilization that NAO sought were difficult to achieve given the changes already underway and the infrequency, the low intensity, and the restricted scope of the treatment they undertook. The problems facing urban areas like Northeast Austin may be beyond the reach of block watch alone to affect.

The Back of the Yards neighborhood was also facing demographic and economic changes; the Council, however, was less amenable to the block watch strategy than NAO. Our survey of residents found fewer positive results in Back of the Yards a year after the program was implemented than in the Northeast Austin area. The Council's goal of service was best achieved by meeting the needs of its constituents, the social, religious, business and educational organizations which comprised its membership. Organizing residents on a block by block basis was inconsonant with the ideology and structure of the Council. As a result, they implemented their crime prevention program in a way that was more compatible with their organization.

The crime program director for the Back of the Yards used group settings, such as meetings with seniors and with youths in local schools, to make presentations about crime. Although this strategy allowed him to reach area residents (who indicated in our survey that they knew about the crime program and were participating in it), it did not allow the meeting participants themselves to do very much about crime. There is some indication, in fact, that fear of crime increased more dramatically in Back of the Yards than in the other areas in our study. Perhaps if you tell residents about area crime problems, but do not provide them with an adequate way to respond to it, you increase the fear and anxiety which already exists.

The crime project director also went door–to–door in the effort to organize watches, but he found great resistance by residents to meet with other block residents. It appeared that his "block watch reps" found more security in their connection to him and to the Council than to their fellow residents. The Council crime director said he did organize seventeen block watches in his target area, however. At one meeting we attended, the central theme was that it was very difficult to trust anyone in the world today.

> The meeting got underway. A young man was telling Ben that their main problem had been some stolen cars this last year. Ben said he would mention this to the police. Ben spoke highly of the new neighborhood relations sergeant and another man said, "You mean the Mexican?" Ben said, yes, that he was very helpful. Ben also mentioned the new commander there named O'Hara. The six people present did not live on the block where the meeting was being held. They all lived on the same block nearby. The reason for this had to do with the fact that this house was available. A woman, commenting on police in the area said, "When Mayor Daley was mayor, they were coming down in droves." A man replied that the police were "doing a good job for the men that they got."

> At this point, Ben explained what a phone tree was. He said everyone on the block would have his own name and phone number on the tree. He called it a "chain of safety." He said it was a "proven fact" that with more people calling, the police were more likely to respond faster. Someone mentioned the inci-

dent on Damen and 49th where the police failed to respond for forty–five minutes when a woman's house was being robbed. This story made the Chicago papers.

Ben then pulled out a sheet with an ABC Crime Poll that Arthur Sims had sent out and began to read some of the statistics about crime which it mentioned. He noted that one person out of ten is a victim of crime in America and that four people out of ten in black neighborhoods are victims of crime. Ben pointed out that since they live near a black neighborhood, that statistic was relevant to them. Then he noted that one out of twelve persons is murdered in the United States. Ben said that murder tended to happen between people who knew each other, so that even among people they know, they needed to be on guard. Ben mentioned some of the crime problems that older people are particularly vulnerable to including con games, and purse snatching; he also mentioned the prevalence of "husband and wife beating" in their district. He said, "You never know—could be a close friend who might assault you." Ben then passed around the block watch map and phone tree and people began putting their names and phone numbers on it.

Ben handed out a sheet about "Crime Prevention Tips" which he got from the police department. He mentioned the business visits that he did each month. He also mentioned that the parks had been pretty safe, but when someone mentioned Sherman park, Ben agreed there had been some incidents there and that the park is "98 percent black." Ben also talked about security when driving which included keeping the windows in your car rolled up and the doors locked, as well as women keeping their purses under their seats. Ben mentioned one incident in which some youths broke the window on the passenger side as a woman was waiting for a light to change and took her purse. Ben also handed out a sheet on "How to Cope with Intruders." Ben mentioned that people should eventually call him after things have settled down, but they should call the police as soon as they can. He emphasized that he is not a "law enforcement officer." Ben handed out a sheet on "United We Stand" which discussed burglary, theft, and assault.

Ben ended the evening by trying to drive home the point about not trusting other people. He used the example of some young women at a mall who saw a woman sitting on a bench crying. They went over to find out what was wrong and the young woman said she and her husband had just had this big fight and she had no way to get home. They offered to give her a lift. On the way, they stopped for gas and the driver decided to phone her husband to tell him she would be late. He was concerned about the person they had picked up and told her to give the woman money to take a cab and to get the woman out of the car. They tried to get her out of the car but she refused. Finally, the police came and moved her. She turned out to be a man dressed in drag and he was carrying a hatchet. This story sent a shock through Ben's listeners. Next he told about a young girl who was kidnapped at a mall when her mother turned around for just a minute. The woman ran up to the security guards and they ordered the mall doors shut. They eventually found a couple with the child, but they had already taken her into a bathroom and shaved her head and dressed her up as a boy. On this note, Ben ended the meeting.

The Council's crime program director also regularly checked with area businesses to see that they were getting an adequate police response to their problems. In all this, the Council was pursuing its goals by providing services and seeking institutional responsiveness for its constituents. It attempted to downplay crime as an issue in the area, and to play up the area's positive virtues. There were two problems with this strategy, however. On the one hand, the Council, more preservation–oriented than it was when it began, but with an organizational structure which did not allow direct membership participation, could be underestimating the fears and anxieties which residents were experiencing. Continued "white flight" and residential transition were the likely result, although it was clear that the Council still remained a visible "presence" and formidable force that many area residents relied on and trusted. On the other hand, there was a whole new set of residents in the area, primarily Hispanics, who had little relationship with or trust in the Council. By failing to integrate these new residents into its organization, the Council could be undermining the base of popular support which made it a force to be reckoned with throughout the years. Thus, even though the block watch strategy alone may be inadequate to affect deep–seated economic and demographic changes, its weak implementation in the Back of the Yards may account for some of the negative results we found one year after the program began. These included an increase in victimization experiences, an increase in youth disorder, a significant increase in the fear of personal and property crime, a decrease in optimism about the neighborhood, and an increase in the likelihood of moving. If our criticism of the block watch program thus far is that the frequency, dosage, and resultant behavioral changes are insufficient to greatly affect notable urban changes, we also may question whether the lack of opportunity for residents to respond in a "collective" manner to changes which seem beyond their control is desirable either.

The areas served by the Edgewater Community Council and the Auburn–Gresham Community Action Coalition were comparatively more stable than those served by NAO and Back of the Yards Council. These were also the two areas that failed to implement a block watch program to any significant degree. Due to the lack of consensus about the goals of its crime program and the absence of a skilled community organizer, the Edgewater Community Council established only one block watch during the period of our observations. Yet, according to our survey, the Council was clearly visible to residents in the target area, and residents reported an increased belief in the efficacy of block action, a decrease in youth disorders, and an increased optimism about the neighborhood. The only significant negative finding on our survey was a decrease in the percent of victimizations reported to the police over the year. This was a neighborhood which perhaps felt itself on the upswing after years of perceived deterioration. Even before the crime program began, our survey of residents found that they were more likely than Chicago city residents as a whole to say that they felt a part of their neighborhood and almost 83 percent said they expected their neighborhood to be better or about the same in two years. The area targeted for the block watch program, which was west of Broadway, included residents concerned about "preservation" and upgrading and redeveloping the Kenmore–Winthrop area. It did not include the lake-fronters to whom crime may have been a more salient issue or the residents of the Kenmore–Winthrop strip who had pressing needs for housing and social services. Although a block watch program was never implemented to any significant degree in this west of Broadway area, we found almost as many positive, significant outcomes and fewer negative outcomes for this area as we did for the area served by the Northwest Neighborhood Federation. Not implementing the program did not appear to hurt this Edgewater neighborhood relative to its control group and the city as a whole; whether not implementing the program actually benefitted the neighborhood cannot be deduced from our data. The Council clearly was a presence in the neighborhood and a source of services and resources for local residents. Residents perhaps were confident that the Kenmore–Winthrop strip was being successfully redeveloped and that the Council was attending to other local problems. This may have held greater weight for them than the fact that they were somewhat more likely than Chicago residents as a whole (24.7 percent to 17.1 percent) to think that crime had increased in the year before the program began. Overall, this appeared to be an optimistic neighborhood which was bullish on it own future.

The Auburn–Gresham community was also bullish. Here, in a solidly black working–class community, 84.3 percent of the residents said they felt a part of their neighborhood, and 94 percent said their neighborhood would be better or the same in two years. Despite this strong base it had to work on, the Auburn–Gresham Community Action Coalition was resource-poor in a neighborhood which had both development and security needs. The requirement of matching the Ford funding meant that the only paid staff person in the organization (the crime program director) spent a lot of his time writing grant proposals and complying with other administrative requirements. The area did have a history of block club organizing, and despite the almost complete lack of implementation of a crime program during the period of our observations, our survey found that residents knew about the Coalition's crime program, had increased their home protection behaviors over the year, were more likely to ask neighbors to watch their homes, and believed there was a decrease in neighborhood deterioration over the year. Our survey turned up no negative findings.

This organization, of the five we studied, had the fewest resources to bring needed services into the area. The crime program director saw the importance of linking crime prevention with insurance rates, and to organizing the community around a number of issues, including housing, health, and education. The crime prevention program, intended to integrate and stabilize urban neighborhoods, was relevant to Auburn–Gresham because of the community's need to involve residents in the solution to a host of problems which affected their safety and security. The lack of opportunity to implement such a program in the area may also be counted among the program's failures.

*Conclusion*

Three observations about the block watch experiences of these five community organizations can be made. First, of the three organizations that actually implemented a block watch program to any significant degree, that is, the Northwest Neighborhood Federation, the Northeast Austin Organization, and the Back of the Yards Neighborhood Council, the Federation implemented the program most successfully; it was also the area in which our survey revealed the most positive and fewest negative program results one year after the "treatment" began. The Northwest Neighborhood Federation undertook the fullest and most complete block watch program and their efforts apparently had some beneficial effects.

Secondly, however, even in this case of successful implementation, the results were disappointing. The majority of findings on our survey in this neighborhood were either nonsignificant or significant in the direction opposite to that hypothesized. We suggested here, as Rosenbaum has elsewhere, that we may have unrealistic expectations for the intervention. Can a few meetings, some increased surveillance, and increased citizen activity redirect large–scale economic and demographic changes within urban neighborhoods? Is block watch alone sufficient? On the other hand, in neighborhoods which were already undergoing deep–seated changes (such as NAO and BYNC), but in which the program was only moderately or weakly implemented, we found the fewest positive outcomes and the most negative outcomes on our survey. This leads us to suggest that even if block watch alone is not sufficient to affect urban changes, its lack of implementation may not be desirable either.

Finally, this leaves us with the two neighborhoods which did not implement the programs to any significant degree, but in which we found more positive findings and fewer negative findings than we did for the areas served by the Northeast Austin Organization and the Back of the Yards Neighborhood Council. We have conjectured that for the Edgewater and Auburn–Gresham areas, comparative neighborhood stability and past community organizing effort lent an optimistic edge to residents' perceptions, despite the lack of implementation of a block watch program. For the Auburn–Gresham Community Action Council, however, the lack of opportunity to participate in such a program should be counted among the program's failings. Here was a neighborhood that needed increased resources and resident involvement to ameliorate problems that affected long–term neighborhood security; the block watch program could have been an effective vehicle to undertake that mobilization.

In sum, therefore, we may say that successful program implementation helped to produce some real gains, but that the program itself may not be sufficient to deal with the magnitude and complexity of urban change. On the other hand, not having the opportunity to participate in such a program may not be an attractive option, either. There can be little doubt that block watch is a popular approach to community crime prevention. However, the data presented here have stimulated us to critically examine this strategy and its empirical and theoretical foundation (see Rosenbaum, Lewis & Grant, 1986; Rosenbaum, 1987). We believe that the theoretical underpinnings of this collective strategy are questionable in several respects and should be reconsidered. Theoretical problems exist at many levels, including the level of implementation, as well as the various levels of predicting effects.

There are other concerns about this type of community crime prevention that we have not addressed, but which are equally troublesome. One of the biggest problems in this area is the paucity of hard evidence that watch programs can stimulate local residents to engage in the types of behaviors that are necessary to strengthen informal social control and reduce the opportunities for criminal behavior (cf. Rosenbaum, 1987). Documented increases in neighborhood surveillance, social interaction, bystander intervention, and specific crime prevention behaviors *as a result* of block watch-type interventions are extremely rare.

In the next chapter, we will try to account for the outcomes we have observed here. We must look to the structure of opportunity within each organization, for it is here that we will find the processes which create these outcomes.

# 8

# Community Organizations and Reform

The conceptual problems of community crime prevention were compounded by the organizational dilemmas each group faced in implementing the block watch. To understand the behavior of these community organizations, we need to come to terms with the priorities that drove their leadership and how each of the groups was organized to pursue its goals. As discussed earlier, the two primary objectives of community organizations are maintenance and political development. By the former, we refer to the preservation of the organization through the recruitment and acquisition of needed members and resources; by the latter, we mean the articulation and pursuit of the critical issues which concern the organization and its constituents.

Block watch can be seen through the prism of these two goals. Indeed, the extent to which block watch is attempted depends on whether organizational maintenance and political development are perceived to be augmented by the activity. In particular, it is *how* a group articulates its goals and how it organizes itself to pursue them that will determine the implementation of the crime prevention initiative.

CIS tried to assist in the implementation process but they concentrated on building commitments to goals, rather than creating a framework for collaborative day–to–day actions that made sense in terms of the ideology and structure of each group. By separating policy formation from implementation as evinced in the Steering Committee and Project Directors' Committee, CIS reduced the likelihood of successful implementation, even for those groups which were structurally predisposed to block watch. However, CIS's "coordinating" posture also reduced the dependency of the community organizations on CIS and allowed the groups independence in operation.

Block watch activity was incorporated or rejected to the extent that it was complementary to the ideology and organization of the group expected to implement the program in exchange for the funding. Where that ideology and organization fit the requirements of the block watch, the group absorbed the program into its operation and proceeded to implement the watches in good faith. When there was a conflict between the block watch and the ideology and organization of the group, the group was not capable of full implementation for it would have undermined the group's political development and caused confusion and disorientation. Community organizations define and articulate issues. That ideology and their capacity to produce collective goods are what they offer the communities they purport to represent. The leadership of these groups will not give up that action orientation easily and they will only supplement it to the extent that the organization benefits from the additional activity.

Incentivists emphasize an organization's ability to translate member preferences into benefits. Dependency theorists emphasize a group's ability to perceive the interests of those members as distinct from those preferences and direct the group to the pursuit of class interests. The former position makes the "amplification" of those preferences primary, while the latter emphasizes presentation of a way to see society and an action orientation to change it. Political development includes both aspects of the rival paradigms but suggests they interact to produce the way an organization articulates an issue. If we are to grasp why each of the CIS groups reacted as it did to the block watch, we must look at how each group amplified member preferences, that is, how they were organized and what ideology shaped the group's direction. The fusion of a group's structure and ideology helps to account for an organization's behavior.

Following Greenstone and Peterson (1976), the primary dimension of ideological variation among the CIS groups varied between preserving the social structure or changing those arrangements to improve the position of subordinate groups. Community organizations schooled in the Alinsky traditions (as all five of the CIS groups were) see themselves as operating along this preservation–change dimension. Those organizations which see their communities as superordinate seek to preserve that position through political activity, and those that see themselves as subordinate seek to change their position. Indeed, as a group achieves success in changing the distribution of benefits, the group's ideology will likely shift to a more preservationist position.

At the same time, each community group must respond to members' concerns. The key dimension here is the extent to which a process exists for translating member preferences into organizational goals. Of course, all community organizations refer to themselves as democratic and go through formal democratic procedures for selecting their leadership, but they vary significantly in their capacity to actually translate member preferences systematically into group activities. The ability to do this depends on a great many factors, but organizations differ depending on how truly democratic they are. The very issues a group focuses on are shaped by their capacity to reflect member preferences. Those groups that have a process for reflecting member interests in political goals we define as participatory democracies. Those that do not are classified as representative or elitist democracies.

The central issue in the political development of community organizations is how the ideological and organizational dimensions fuse and create the particular context for action, in this case, around the crime issue. An organization that facilitates member preferences must then be comfortable with the priorities that may emerge for the group. These preferences may not be in harmony with the ideological goals of the leadership. Conversely, the ideological interests of the leadership may shape organizational goals at the cost of some members who are not persuaded by their analysis.

A group's orientation to social change, particularly whether its leadership emphasizes preservation or redistribution of values, will make crime a more or less attractive issue. This follows from a definition of crime as a conservative issue, that is, an issue that focuses on preservation and maintenance of privilege rather than redistribution and change. To develop programs and activities about crime is to support the status quo and keep intruders and strangers out.

Groups with a preservationist ideology and participatory structure would be best suited to a block watch program because the amplification of member preferences are likely to coincide with the leadership's own preferences. Conversely, groups with a social change ideology and elitist structure would be ill–suited to a block watch program because the group's leaders are likely to define crime as an issue not in their membership's true interests. Groups with a preservationist ideology and elitist structure and groups with a social change ideology and participatory structure would fall in between. While having some affinity for the program, they are not likely to be fully committed to it either because it would conflict with how they make decisions or raise issues not consonant with the leadership's preferences.

Each of the five groups in our study mixed ideology and organization in different ways. All the groups were democratic in a formal sense. Each organization recruited its leadership and set its priorities through democratic procedures. These procedures were routinized and voting was the mechanism for selection. Most of the groups had yearly conventions at which members chose the major issues for the coming year. The Board of Directors of each organization was responsible to the membership for its behavior, and the staffs were responsible to the volunteer leadership. The groups varied tremendously, however, in the extent to which there were mechanisms for actually operationalizing member concerns. Some groups worked hard to recruit members whose preferences could shape the organization's priorities. These preferences could shape local activities directly and be communicated up the hierarchy to shape the overall direction of the organization. This participatory approach is not without its costs in both time and conflict. People see things differently and have different interests. Accommodating these differences takes effort and some may not be pleased with the outcome of those deliberations. Crime is an obvious example. But the organizations that stimulate grass–roots representation have a better chance of representing member interests in organizational priorities.

Groups that relied on members' preferences to generate organizational activity were then confined to these preferences. For preservationist organizations, leaders were likely to be comfortable with participatory procedures for they did not need to move members away from their narrow self–interests. For social change organizations, however, leaders might not feel entirely comfortable with member preferences, as they were likely to move the organization away from what leaders saw as critical political goals.

Other groups set their organization's agenda from the top. The leadership would generate priorities and pursue them. Often there were no mechanisms for member ratification, and if members disapproved, their only recourse was to exit the organization or bite their tongues. These groups rely on their leadership's sense of what is best for the group. Dependency theorists do not see this as a problem, for as the leaders pursue group goals, they "educate" their members, and to the extent that their analysis is correct, it will win over the recalcitrant.

If this analysis is correct, the block watch intervention is best suited to the preservationist, participatory group on two counts. First, it creates a format for member preferences to be voiced and pursued on a local ad hoc basis. What the block watch meeting decides are the priorities for the block; it can pursue these (within limits) independent of the larger organization. Second, the block watch offers an organizational mechanism for linking members in a bottom–up agenda setting format. Block watches send representatives to meetings in which block preferences are represented to the broader group, and through which the preferences of others can be communicated back to the block. The Northwest Neighborhood Federation had both the ideology (preservationist) and the structure (participatory) to make the block watch a reasonable activity to which to commit. The program suited both their maintenance and political development needs.

Those organizations that supported a social change ideology found less comfort in the block watch idea. It offered little in the way of legitimacy for an agenda to redistribute resources to lower income communities, much less a mechanism through which lower class communities could remedy injustices at the hands of city agencies. NAO and Auburn–Gresham were the two groups in our sample with social change orientations, although both organizations also had concerns about preservation. Both organizations were nominally participatory in structure, but in practice much of the impetus for each organization's priorities came from its leadership. Auburn–Gresham, though the least developed politically, had a lot to work with organizationally. The community was rich in block *clubs,* many of which had sprung up independently of the community group, but were affiliated. These groups were perfect units for watch activities if the club members could be convinced of the utility of the activity and they were not already informally engaged in the behaviors. Ironically, this group, which was structurally predisposed to the program, was dropped (or forced to leave) for other administrative reasons. While crime was not the top priority of this group's leadership, the block watch program could have served a source of member recruitment and been marginally useful to it in terms of political development. NAO, while comfortable with the concept of block watch both as an organizing tool and as one mechanism for coping with crime, incorporated the block watch into its routine method of operation. For this group, the watch met both recruitment needs and some of the political goals of the organization. In both cases, however, the basic adherence to a social change ideology combined with limited access to member preferences made the leaders of these two groups less than eager to invest a lot of time and energy into a program which did not seem to offer *major* political benefits.

The Back of the Yards Neighborhood Council and the Edgewater Community Council were more elitist in structure than the other groups; these two organizations were primarily oriented to neighborhood preservation. For these two groups, a block watch program that would amplify member preferences would run counter to the established mechanisms already in place for articulating organizational agendas. BYNC operated through a substantive committee structure and an annual convention and was not particularly interested in creating new units for expressing citizen concerns. Small, turf–based units would conflict with the organization's existing decision–making structure. In addition, though the organization had now become preservation–oriented, the group's leaders were concerned about maintaining the group's reputation both with residents and the public at large and were therefore not receptive to a program that would focus too much attention on crime. ECC faced a similar dilemma about block watch. On the one hand, new units of organization would compete with ones already in place for the loyalty of members. Moreover, there were two subconstituencies within the organization which had different, but shared, objections to making crime a major local issue that the organizations needed to address. In these two cases, block watch was not a significant recruitment tool, nor did it help these groups to develop their political agendas in a way that felt comfortable to its leadership.

The affinity for a block watch program thus materializes within community organizations as a result of intraorganizational conditions. Both how a group chose to amplify member preferences and what the major orientation of its leadership was determined how receptive a group was to the goals of the block watch program as articulated by CIS. For groups like the Northwest Neighborhood Federation, the program fit well with their organizational aim of amplifying resident concerns and with the leadership's preference for preserving the community's position in the competition for metropolitan benefits. NAO and Auburn–Gresham were structurally predisposed to the program, but the organizations' leaders were ambivalent about the political benefits of the program. On the other hand, Back of the Yards Neighborhood Council and the Edgewater Community Council were not structurally predisposed to the program, and while their leadership could not ignore residents' concerns about crime, they themselves were not particularly receptive to an opportunity reduction model which circumvented the established criminal justice institutions and which threatened the reputations of the communities.

Thus, in considering a program like block watch, judging the program on its crime prevention merits alone (which have now been seriously called into question) may not be sufficient to explain a community organization's receptiveness to implementing the program. We have argued that a program like block watch needs to be seen within the ideological and structural context of each organization and whether the program furthered the maintenance and political development needs of the group. Those groups with a preservationist ideology and participatory structure (like the Northwest Neighborhood Federation) were most predisposed to a block watch program because it could further their maintenance and political development needs. Those organizations with a social change orientation and an elitist structure would be least receptive to such a program, and perhaps not surprisingly, we had no such group in our sample. This leaves us with groups then that may either be structurally or ideologically predisposed to the program, but the conflict between these elements produces a less than full commitment to program implementation. NAO and Auburn–Gresham were structurally receptive to the program, but ideologically ambivalent. On the other hand, Back of the Yards Neighborhood Council and Edgewater Community Council were not structurally predisposed to the program, although their leadership was concerned about neighborhood preservation. In all, the fusion of ideological and structural conditions with the maintenance and political development needs of an organization largely determined willingness to make a full commitment to program implementation.

# 9

# The Ironies of Communal Strategies
# to Prevent Crime

On the cover of a CIS handbook on block watch is a quote from Jane Jacobs, *Death and Life of Great American Cities:*

> The first thing to understand is that the public peace . . . is not kept primarily by the police, necessary as police are. It is kept primarily by an intricate, almost unconscious, network of voluntary controls and standards among the people themselves. . . . No amount of police can enforce civilization where the normal casual enforcement of it has broken down.

The quotation is shorthand rationale for the strategy of block watch which is described and promoted in the pages of the manual and which was the focus of their Ford grant. The obvious message is that the way to promote the public peace is to reestablish that "civilization" where it has broken down and the block watch is a way of doing that.

Following the lead of virtually all community crime prevention programs, the Citizen Information Service placed *crime reduction* and *fear reduction* at the top of its list of program goals. However, the most important goal, and one that underlies most organizing efforts, was to *build a sense of community.* There is much talk among practitioners and academics about the importance of organizing efforts for maintaining and enhancing social cohesion or social integration in the community. They share a hope for the urban neighborhood where residents interact on a regular basis, share a common set of norms about social behavior, and identify with the neighborhood as a desirable place to live.

To build that sense of community, residents had to be "empowered" through collective action. Almost by definition, community organization works to empower local residents and to give them a sense of efficacy with regard to changes in their neighborhood.

How does a community organization achieve the goals of reducing crime, reducing fear of crime, enhancing social cohesion and empowering the residents of the neighborhood? The most fundamental process is "community organizing" for the purpose of stimulating "collective action." By distributing information to community residents (in person, by phone, or by mail) and by arranging local meetings, hopefully citizens are brought together to address local problems and take collective action.

Block watch through opportunity reduction and informal social control would build community. Opportunity reduction means that when the surveillance and reporting of suspicious activities by residents is increased, potential offenders perceive an increased risk of detection and apprehension, and therefore, are deterred from committing offenses. Informal social control restricts crime and disorder by enforcing informal standards and controls which the community holds. The expectation for community crime prevention is that organizers will stimulate the types of social interaction necessary to strengthen social bonds and enhance social cohesion.

The block watch suggests that such a peace has mysterious roots, that it develops out of attachments which are not rational and may find their origins in the tribal sentiments which predate modern society. That peace follows from what some call primary relations, that is, associations of family and kin which create deep feelings which are the building blocks of solidarity and community. If it is in fact the case that its origins and foundations are complex, this suggests two things about efforts to reproduce it. First, once this web has been broken it will be difficult to replace and second, its sources lie in intricate emotional relationships. The latter point suggests that reform efforts should work best in those communities which share values and long–term attachments, the areas least likely to need help, if the analysis is correct.

Peace follows rather mysteriously from consensus. While few would quarrel with this formulation, for it is true by definition, the difficulties begin when we ask how that consensus originates and what might be done to bring it into existence once it has dissolved. Normative order could certainly be equated with peace, but this definitional trick hardly accounts for its inception where people do not participate in that order.

If Jacobs' approach is correct, the criminal justice system plays a secondary role in the production of peace. The police as well as other agencies cannot enforce peace where normative consensus is absent. Police courts and corrections cannot possibly foster conformity if the underlying connections are not already in place. This world of secondary relations cannot replace the solidarity of primary attachments. Where community is absent, coercion will fail. But if community is absent, why will people join the block watch effort? And even more importantly, should the police, courts and corrections be dismissed so easily, given the legitimacy of state action and our lack of other enforcement tools?

A secure community derives from primordial relations. The government and the public arena of which it is a part are unimportant. There is no distinct realm of discourse and experience in which problems of order and security can be solved. Lofland (1982) in a slightly different context puts the problem nicely, when she notes that public culture and civilized political conflict cannot flourish when there is little understanding of the importance of public discourse as a distinct arena for human interaction. Ironically, community crime prevention withdraws from the world of politics, planning and the public interest.

It is this *communal perspective* which has been both the source of the block watch (and community crime prevention) appeal and the core of its weakness. The theorists of community crime prevention develop this theme to the detriment of the communities they hope to help. These critics of American society replace "economic" man and the individualism which supports his ascendence with "communal man" and an ideology of community which will restore the sense of solidarity and belonging which has been eroded by urban capitalistic society.

Communal man lives in a world of private relations which, while depleted by modern life, is the bedrock of collective action. Block watch activities take those private needs (attachment) and interests (security) and use them to stimulate common action. Working outside of the state's legitimate attempts to control crime (police, courts, etc.) and without legitimacy itself (no government authority), the community organization fosters collective action in between the public and private realms. The directly political work of intervening government actions is eschewed for community building.

While the public peace may in fact rely on shared values, where that public peace does not exist those values have not served to promote tranquility. It may be descriptively correct that peace flows from informal social networks. The prescription which follows from this understanding is deceptively simple and incorrect. Creating community is not the same as reforming a community. Peace is more the expression of an integrated society, rather than the source of that integration (Hammond, 1980). Reformers who try to create the ties which never existed or have eroded over time will have a tall order, given the limited political and economic resources available to the groups involved. Indeed if the social forces of urban capitalism are as potent as most reformers believe, there is little hope they will be transcended by strategies which depend on people rejecting their individualistic and selfish "bourgeois interiors" for a deeper more communal commitment outside the worlds of government authority and action.

Community crime prevention will not achieve its goals because it has made the wrong assumptions about human behavior and misjudged how people will respond to the programs offered. A sound critique of American individualism is not the same thing as a good road map to action. A moving analysis of what is wrong with ourselves and society is not the same thing as a strategy to change it. This is precisely the problem with community approaches to social reform in criminology. They tap a need felt in most of us for more of a sense of belonging, but they do not describe how we will respond to our environment of which they become a part as a consequence of reform efforts. We can see through the analysis the limits of policing and a reliance on self interest as ways to combat crime in cities and that leads us to an alternative approach to crime prevention which relies on building community to create conformity. This approach in turn suggests that community organizations are the vehicle for socializing people into the value system of the community and that secondary institutions are ill-equipped for this job. But the critique is built on a notion that communal man is hiding within economic man and that he will respond to the call to restore himself through community. The problem is that he rarely does. The impact of a complex urban society has transformed who he is. One's occupation, where one lives, how one's children are educated, the mass media, all these sectors of life demand that one think in terms of individual self interest and economic priorities. We may not like aspects of ourselves and our lives but our tools for change are given in our institutions and culture. To hope that in the area of crime prevention we will start to act differently and that those actions will pay off in increased solidarity and security is to underestimate the overall impact of the very system which is seen as being so destructive. Everything we have become will not be put aside because a meeting had been called to improve the crime situation. The self which has emerged as both a coping mechanism and an expression of who we are would be transformed with the advent of community crime prevention.

Since people will still calculate their benefits and costs when it comes to the use of their time and energy and since the participation of citizens is voluntary in these crime prevention efforts, there can be little doubt that for many who do not share the sense of loss of community which may motivate some, the *effectiveness* of the operation will be of paramount importance. For those with other agenda, like personal aggrandizement and political ambition, there will be reasons to stay involved because of the platform the program may give them both within the community organization and in the community at large. But for most, the program has to be a benefit they would not receive without participation.

Our economic man or woman will quickly tire of the meetings and phone calls and surveillance of the street if something does not accrue to him or her for the effort. More abstractly, as he listens to the proposals from the organization about getting involved in the enterprise, he will process the plan through the prism he usually uses to think through crime problems. For most of us, this means thinking about crime as a problem for the police and associated with the purposes and interests of those who violate the law. Each of us has a theory of crime causation and most of us believe in personal responsibility for ourselves and others. Most hold that evil men act criminally and the police are responsible for finding them and punishing them. We avoid crime by taking precautions and staying away from people we don't trust. We hope that our commitments to individual responsibility and economic rationality will be preserved by the state. Reform efforts which deny this heritage will usually fail in this complex, highly individualistic culture.

The block watch approach is an implicit critique of American individualism. It draws a picture of communal life which assumes an "undersocialized" view of human nature in which we can become something different. Usually both political legitimacy and social pathology find their sources in the individual. Most crime prevention strategies begin with the individuals as the source of the crime problem. Attempts to remedy that crime problem begin with changing the person. That change or prevention process often diagnoses and classifies the factors that produce criminal behavior in the individual. The social science community has often taken exception to this orientation and suggested that the group rather than the person ought to be the starting place for understanding human behavior and criminality. This is true both for the causes of the problem and for the proposed solutions. Theories that arise with individualistic assumptions place the blame for the problem squarely on the shoulders of the person who is committing the criminal act. Solutions that follow from this assumption also seek to change those individuals and often leave unexamined the institutions through which people act. Scholars writing in the block watch tradition have attempted to shift the debate to the forces outside the individual that shape behavior. Crime prevention rests then on changing communities rather than controlling the individuals who violate the law.

CIS followed much scholarly opinion and suggested that community crime prevention (and block watch) can be used not only to reduce crime and its negative effects on the community, but also to empower the local residents so that they can more fully participate in American society. Community organizations can use crime prevention to achieve reform. Crime prevention can help in both that general process and with the local crime problems. The content of the crime prevention activity itself has drawn less attention than the consequences of bringing the community resident into the prevention process. Block watch itself was less important than the agent of change, the community organization, and the empowerment of

local people through their own organizations. The block watch was assumed to be useful and took its meaning from the fact that the groups
themselves were bringing residents together. Sims himself acknowledges
that it was his reading of the crime prevention field, rather than direct
experience with block watch that led him to suggest this strategy for the
groups. With the important exception of NNF, none of the groups nor CIS
knew how to run a competent block watch program.

CIS and the groups were naive about the difficulties of grafting a new
program onto living organizations. Many of the groups were quite critical
of the police and saw the block watch as a way to function independently to
provide security. Some of the organizers saw the watch as a way to challenge
the police monopoly on security and bring the citizens more actively into
this realm to produce their own sense of efficacy and security.

The block watch approach could assist the group in developing alternative ways of thinking about security and offer ways to present the organization as having a central role in crime prevention. By relying on the police
for protection the group would both explicitly and implicitly give approval
to the ways decisions were made about crime prevention and the content of
those decisions for the community. If the groups were to challenge the
status quo and deal themselves into the policy process in a serious way, they
must avoid giving the present arrangements their approval and putting
themselves in the position of supporting policies that leave the community
out of the decisionmaking process.

Some analysts think that the block watch approach is the only way to
deal community groups into the policy arena in ways that could lead to a
redistribution of resources with the community enhancing its position in
the decisionmaking process. Community strategies like block watch lead to
the making of political demands, and police strategies lead to accommodation with the status quo. The CIS block watch approach was intended to
empower. It allowed the groups to demonstrate to the community that
involvement with the group had benefits which enhanced security and
improved the community. It sought a method of improving the community
that did not depend on the police, although the police do have to respond
to the demands of the blocks that are organized. If a community employs
the block watch idea they will, by their own efforts, make the community
safer. That approach makes the police and other units of government more
responsive, which in turn improves the situation even more.

The ultimate dilemma of block watch in the current case is that the
community ideology moved the organizations away from directly confronting political issues around crime and politics. Making the political
demands that would have improved the capacity of the groups to articulate
their politics and pursue objectives that would have gained membership

and increase legitimacy among community residents and city leaders had to be done through the back door. The emphasis on building primary relations kept the groups from directly pursuing political objectives. The depoliticized approach served the academic and philanthropic constituencies and gave the middle-class reform group a way of going about their business that looked non-partisan, but the result was to shift the group away from the political development they sought. Community organizations can and will retain and recruit members and they will do this through a combination of incentives that work.

Block watch fails to meet the needs of the groups for political development, for it does not take into consideration the particular organization and ideology that each group has developed over time. As each group (except NNF) goes about the business of implementing the block watch it confronts the structure of its own development. CIS was in the uncomfortable role of stimulating differential responses to the crime problem based on the perspectives of the groups involved, but at the same time pursuing block watch. This led to much discussion of the goals of the block watch, but little day to day help in getting the watches off the ground for that might be seen as intrusion.

The democratic principle which treats crime prevention as something that can be done independent of government institutions and social scientific thinking does avoid the problem of cooptation and goal deflection, at least in the abstract; but it faces at least in this case the equally troubling dilemma of isolation and goal deflection.

Reform, we have argued, is the result of negotiations and accommodations between and within the organizations. Those "pragmatic interactions" are shaped by the interests and ideologies of the actors involved, and the compromises associated with the clash of differing perspectives and objectives. Block watch meant something different to each community organization depending on its ideology and organizational structure. In some groups (NNF) fit comfortably with the organization, while in others it served no useful purpose. Where it did "fit," block watch helped the group pursue the recruitment of members and agenda-setting procedures. Thus the theory of communal man which drives block watch and community crime prevention in general, while attractive to reformers at CIS and in some community groups, played little role in the acceptance or rejection of the strategy. Rather, each group assessed the utility of the block watch as a tool for the enhancement of the organization and adapted it to the group's structure and perspective.

CIS tried to assist in the implementation process but they concentrated on building commitments to goals rather than creating a framework for collaborative day-to-day actions. By separating policy formation from

implementation as evinced in the Steering Committee and a project director committee, CIS reduced the likelihood of implementation especially
for those structurally predisposed (NAO and Auburn–Gresham) to the
block watch. However, their "coordinating" posture also reduced the dependency of the community organizations on CIS and allowed the groups
independence in operation.

Several authors have suggested that community crime prevention can be
used not only to reduce crime and its negative effects on the community,
but also to empower the local residents so that they can more fully participate in American society. Community organizations can energize the dis-
possessed to achieve a larger share of the American pie through democratic
political action. Crime prevention can both help in that general process
and with the local crime problems. The content of the crime prevention
activity itself has drawn less attention than the consequences of bringing
the community resident into the prevention process. Actual activities were
less important than the agent of change, the community organization, and
the empowerment of local people in their own organizations.

What the groups decided to do, in this case, the block watch, was less
important in its content and took its meaning from the fact that the groups
themselves had selected this activity. Equally important was the fact that
there was even less understanding of how to coordinate the watch with
other things that the groups were doing in the criminal justice area. The
block watch itself could be operated without much coordination with government agencies and what contact these agencies had came when piece-
meal demands were made for more and better service. This communal or
self–help aspect of the program made it easier to get the activity off the
ground, but limited its effectiveness with law enforcement and municipal
agencies. Many current crime prevention strategies were designed to be
supplemental to law enforcement activities, that is, assist the police, courts,
etc., in performing their duties. Many community organizations work
more closely with the police and other agencies seeing their contribution as
supportive rather than independent. Many of the groups in the project
were quite critical of the police and saw the block watch as a way to develop
independent competence to pursue security. Some of the organizers saw the
watch as a way to challenge the police monopoly on security and bring the
citizens more actively into this realm of government service.

From a political standpoint we can distinguish community strategies
from supplemental strategies and propose that the content of the strategy
might be related to the political development of the organization that does
the activity. Neither the incentivist nor dependency theorists give us much
guidance in how to think of the effect of program substance on political
development. The incentivists suggest that content is neutral and that pro-

ducing benefits for members is more important than the substance of the benefits. The incentivists are also uninterested in content for they believe that the source of the support dictates its impact on political development. In our analysis of the CIS groups, we have suggested that political development and program substance are closely related. How the groups articulate issues will shape how they do crime prevention.

But this process is also interactive, that is, the substance of the activity may affect how the groups in question develop politically. If a group articulates certain ways of going about crime prevention, these ought to be related to how that group sees its own activities and political development. The community approach would allow the group to challenge the status quo both in terms of how the police and other agencies do their jobs and how priorities are established. The community approach could assist the group in developing alternative ways of thinking about security and offer ways to present the organization as having a central role in crime prevention. By relying on the supplemental approaches the group would both explicitly and implicitly give approval to the ways decisions were made about crime prevention and the content of those decisions.

The supplemental approach by its nature leaves the community with no more say in these matters since the group accepts a subsidiary role in the prevention process. Community strategies lead to the making of political demands and supplemental strategies lead to accommodation with the status quo. The CIS block watch approach has all the characteristics of the self–help approach. It allows the groups to demonstrate to the community that involvement with the group has benefits which enhance security and improve the community. It seeks a method of improving the community that does not depend on the police, although the police do have to respond to the demands of the blocks that are organized. If the community employs the block watch idea they will by their own efforts, make the community safer. That approach makes the police and other units of government more responsive, which in turn improves the situation even more.

Supplemental strategies are said to have the opposite effect, for they keep the community passive and reactive to the way the police and other agencies define and work on the issues of security and since the community isn't doing that well under the current situation they will at best maintain the status quo. The ultimate dilemma of the perspective in the current case is that the self–help ideology moved the organizations away from directly confronting the political issues around crime and politics. Making the political demands that would have improved the capacity of the groups to articulate their politics and pursue objectives that would have gained membership and increase legitimacy among community residents and city leaders had to be done through the back door. The emphasis on the collective response that built primary relations kept the groups from directly pursuing political objectives. The depoliticized approach served the academic and philanthropic constituencies and gave the middle–class reform group a way of going about their business that looked non–partisan, but the result was to shift the group away from the political development they sought. Community organizations can and will retain and recruit members and they will do this through a combination of incentives that work. Block watch seems to show little benefit and when it does it is hard to see that it is from the block watch per se. Even more distressing is the reduction of feelings of efficacy among those who got directly involved.

Block watch fails on its face to meet the needs of the groups for political development, for it does not take into consideration the particular organization and ideology that each group has developed over time. As each group goes about the business of implementing the block watch it confronts the sediment of its own development which disallows the implementation process. CIS was in the uncomfortable role of stimulating differential responses to the crime problem based on the perspectives of the groups involved, but at the same time seeking a common ground to work from, namely the block watch. This led to much discussion of what the groups were doing and trying to get them to commit to the goals of the block watch, but provided little day–to–day help in getting the watches off the ground for that might be seen as intrusion.

Marris and Rein were writing twenty years ago about Ford and crime prevention projects and they suggested that, as conceived, the projects could not work. They suggested that for a social reform to have a chance of success, it must involve a powerful coalition, be logically sound and radically democratic. The CIS–Ford project has evolved beyond the earlier formulation of social reform. Indeed of the three elements which were of equal importance twenty years ago, one, radical democracy, has emerged as the most important. Coalitions of powerful actors and institutions usually stalemate each other and the legitimacy of social science is in much debate especially as it relates to government programs and social change. However, the commitment to democracy at least at the Ford Foundation seems to have emerged as the most important value. This would explain how the foundation would fund and support a project that excluded the major institutions of government and was based on very flimsy evidence about the utility of the proposed intervention. The value choice is by no means a bad one, for if the redistribution of power and the support of indigenous movements and articulation of indigenous interests is what you are after, then the delegation of the other two factors to the dust bin of philanthropy seems warranted. It does however leave the groups funded in a somewhat difficult situation, for they are on their own in terms of producing the results they promised. One of the benefits of a coalition and of social science participation is that there is support around for carrying off the project, even if it gets reshaped in the process. CIS and the groups stood by themselves trying to figure out how to do what they had promised and often finding themselves in the names of community working in a vacuum, accomplishing very little by both crime prevention and political development standards.

The community model which treats crime prevention as something that can be done independent of government institutions and social scientific thinking does avoid the problem of cooptation and goal deflection, at least in the abstract; but it faces at least in this case the equally troubling dilemma of isolation and poor results.

The five groups we looked at in this book were moved by the CIS into the community camp. CIS, in its technical assistance, pursued the notion that if they increased the internal democracy of the groups they would improve the capacity of the groups to develop themselves. CIS was very shy of partisan politics and continued to move the groups away from them whenever a move in that direction was suggested. This, coupled with the time and effort that went into the development of the new watches, seemed to take the groups away from their political goals.

At a minimum this discussion suggests that the community ideology in the crime prevention field may not have the effects some of its advocates promise. Community crime prevention may undermine political development and supportive strategies may stimulate it. In the case of the CIS project the results are clear. The communities did not increase their security by doing the block watch and often people who participated in it felt worse about their capacity to affect change at the local level. The organizations themselves were not harmed by their participation and for the most part used the resources to their best advantage. However if the reformers were interested in preventing crime and increasing democracy and equality, they seemed to have selected the wrong approach. There are crime prevention strategies that include the police and facilitate more interactive approaches which have improved the community and reduced some of the negative impacts of crime. From a reform as well as a crime prevention perspective these may prove to be more useful in the long run than what CIS and the community organizations did. This is only one project and we studied it for a year, but the results suggest that those that seek a safer and more just society look beyond community programs to achieve these ends.

# 10

# Community and the Undersocialized View of Man

The concept of community never stands alone. As Bender (1978) and Gusfield (1975) suggest, it is almost always part of a typology in which it is contrasted with noncommunal patterns of life, usually modern urban existence. When community is used in this way, it almost always has a positive connotation. Modern society is negative and community is positive. In historical and sociological studies of crime causation and prevention, modern crime problems are usually produced by rapid social change. As society becomes more complex, crime increases and undermines civil order. Often the modern problems are contrasted with a time when there was less crime, due in large part to the sense of community which flourished then.

The absence of community is employed to explain the negative outcomes of change and to suggest ways to improve the current scene, usually by recreating community. If we can recapture that sense of belonging and attachment, then fewer social problems would emerge. The community organization often plays a central role in the recreation of communal sensibility for it can articulate the needs and interests of those who long for more of a sense of attachment and control.

While almost every period in American history has been described by one scholar or another as the watershed when community was lost (Bender, 1978), there have been few periods in which it has been restored. This has not dampened efforts to try. Indeed one irony of the community perspective is that often the solutions to the crime problem do not attend to the forces which brought about the change in the first place. All the powerful forces which have undone community are swept aside by the citizen's newly found desire for attachment. The heterogeneity of values, the division of labor, the occupational structure, the media and governmental intrusion all lose their impact on the lives of community members when the community organization goes to work. How could a small, weak group of citizens working with few resources and little authority change the course of modern society? Spurred on with help from the welfare state, we now encounter the unusual situation in which government intervention produces community. Some suggest that community can only follow from government funding of community groups, because the latter groups have the capacity to weave people back into a network of attachments which will produce peace and civility. But how will a grant from a foundation or the federal authorities reverse the social forces which undermine community? A longing for attachment and a sense of place must be strong enough to nullify those factors when they were not able to do so before. This approach suggests a definition of human nature in which our communal nature is independent of social and cultural forces. This communal factor is strong enough to assert itself over the socializing influences which have shaped the person but only after community groups get funded. How this communal element survives the onslaught of modernization is not specified.

What is hard to accept about this formulation is not the assumption of a communal instinct (after all, Aristotle and Marx made similar assumptions), but rather that it is powerful enough to generate and sustain activities which go against the grain of modern life. Without this instinct the person would pay little attention to the organization and its notions of restoring community. As Wilson and Herrnstein (1985) suggest in their controversial book, the traditional assumption about human nature is that we are all self–interested calculators. The assumption of economic man is now replaced by "communal man." Since community is transformed into society in the modern era, there must be a residual longing for attachment which motivates the individual to engage in community programs. Heclo (1986) in a different context suggests that most Americans are culturally drawn towards more individualistic approaches to improving their well–being.

> It is a conception of well–being that is supremely individualistic, for it has to do with the capacity of an individual to go his own way, to enjoy the fruits of his own labor, to be unbeholden, unentangled, able to make it on his own.

Community crime prevention posits a set of reform strategies which see welfare improved through collective efforts, strategies which engage citizens with their fellow residents. That solidarity will, in turn, lead to less crime and more political power for those in the community. If we build and fund community, we prevent crime. But it is done together, not individually.

Communal man lives in a world of local ties and mutual dependency, a world in which the government and the public realm in general are at best unimportant for securing order. Economic man, on the other hand, lives in a world of work, laws and individual rationality, a world in which the government has a large, if reactive, role in securing peace and maintaining order. Economic man has accepted market relations and seeks to protect himself within the cultural context which is given.

> Whatever one's perspective, the point is that this individualistic conception of welfare closely corresponds to a regime of both civil liberties and also modern versions of market–oriented, economic rationality. Such economic rationality implies something more specific than the literal meaning of rationality—the making of ratio calculations between means and ends. It is a view that assumes economic rationality is everywhere and always a matter of individual calculations for maximizing individual utility (Heclo, 1987).

By assuming communal man in opposition to economic man, many reformers have lost the ability to see how individualism and market relations shape responses to the crime problem and reform efforts. Purveyors of the community perspective see their strategies as alternatives to conventional measures rather than seeing those measures and the modern society which produced them as the context for collective action.

This communal approach treats individualism as selfishness and egoism and urges citizens to overcome those elements of their personality to achieve community. This latent critique follows from the judgment that the competitiveness and anomie of American life make crime more likely by isolating victims and reducing opportunities for offenders. But by treating community as the obverse of individualism, it treats reforms as cultural critiques rather than cultural adjustments. Since our welfare depends in great measure on our ability to support ourselves and families in labor markets and since we are not bound to local communities in our pursuit of income, the economic realm and the values it generates play a huge role in shaping how we handle crime problems. But the realm of capitalism and its culture are something to be opposed rather than a context for action.

In our society, money buys security, and economic resources produce self–realization (Rainwater, 1974). To ignore this simple cultural fact is to miss the primary importance of economic power. Economic rationality shapes our lives and shapes our choices. Employment is the chief source of income. Work also supplies the sense of identity and worthiness which provides personal satisfaction. Without economic resources most people lack access to validating experiences. Economic self interest guides many of the choices we make about how to spend time. Will it contribute to my welfare? Will it make me more secure? Communal man seeks community, but he cannot achieve it if we all respond individually to the problems we face. The way most people protect themselves is to purchase the distance from criminals that money can buy. We do this through doormen and suburbs. As our income grows, so does our security.

The central point in all this is that a reform strategy must accurately describe well how Americans are likely to act, not simply how we want them to act. In the area of crime prevention and participation the American citizen will by and large act as "self–interested man," looking for ways to maximize benefits and decrease costs. He will not be enthusiastic about crime prevention efforts, for his access to security comes through increased economic well–being and mobility. It's easier to change communities than to make communities change.

Reform efforts which avoid this unpleaseant reality about life in a capitalist country will not attract the interest of those it seeks to help. Those reforms will not further their interests nor will they fit their belief systems. A capitalist culture will breed utilitarians. The culture will provide ways to negotiate the institutions through which one lives and create meaningful experiences for those who seek community and security.

> Now, if culture is an adaptation to life situations, if it is transmitted as the accumulated knowledge of the group about how to adapt, and if the learning of that culture is systematically reinforced by the experiences that individuals have as they grow up and go about their daily lives making their own individual adaptation to their own individual social and ecological situation, then one can predict that any effort to change lower–class culture directly by outside educational intervention is doomed to failure. Lower–class people will have no incentive to change their culture (indeed they would suffer if they tried), unless there is some significant change in their situation (Rainwater, n.d.).

If Americans are self–interested and think by and large in economic terms about who they are and what they want, then communal ideologies will neither persuade nor work as guides to action. They may attract interest because they speak to weaknesses in our culture, but they cannot be alternatives to that culture. This is the fatal flaw in community–oriented reforms. They feed our desire for attachment and community, but offer a faulty program to bring us together. They fail to change the institutions which breed our individualism. Cultures don't change situations; situations change cultures. Undersocialized views of man which urge people to change how they live and solve problems will fail as reforms.

Communal man is a response to economic man. The former is that part of us which has been atrophied by the institutions and demands which surround us. He is the need in us which emerges from a competitive life in a market–oriented society. We wish to be measured by what we can contribute, not just by now much we make. There is another part of us which delights in the freedom and autonomy which the market provides. Community also has a negative connotation, suggesting the manacles of stifling tradition, limited opportunities, and oppressive control by others. Most of us seek a balance, using the limited cultural tools at our disposal to fashion a comfortable attachment which does not imprison us.

Whatever our normative reaction to the communal perspective, the most important level of reaction is participatory. Does the critique and the program elicit cooperation and participation from those it tries to attract? While it may draw in those who want this communal closeness, for others, especially in poor communities, neighbors appear more as a threat than a comfort. While most people seek community through social and family ties, local organizations will appear attractive to some for finding community and taking leadership roles.

Social reforms have to make sense to those who would take part. When someone asks that an effort be made to change the distribution of power in our society he has to argue that the effort is not only practical, but that it furthers some goal the participants seek to achieve. The coercion involved in forcing compliance challenges our democratic principles. Twenty years ago Marris and Rein argued that voluntary participation was essential to implementing social reforms. While there must be a coalition of elites who seek the reform, they must also argue persuasively for the rationality of the effort they seek to embark on. For community crime prevention, that rationality is presented as social science, a set of propositions about how the action contemplated will bring about the changes sought, about how people will be drawn to the effort because of their interests and attitudes, and how the institutions touched by the effort will react. These ideas must do two things if they are to help the reformers. They must ring true to those individuals who will do the reforming and also give a pretty good picture of how people will act, so that the reform has a chance of producing the results it promises. Community crime prevention suffers on both counts.

Social reform must be descriptive and normative. If the picture of reform violates a participant's values about what kind of world he wants and how he believes people behave, he will not get involved. If the reform promises changes which will not benefit the person or the groups to which he belongs, questions will arise about the utility of the efforts and participation. These questions are clearly raised throughout this book. The ideology of community crime prevention may justify local political development but it fails for the most part to offer a workable or meaningful solution to crime problems for most community organizations.

Becker (1967) proposed that social scientists cannot help taking sides in looking at social institutions. He proposes that there is a hierarchy of credibility through which we accept the perspective of those at the top of organizations as the truth about what goes on in the organization in question. The same may be said of the relations between organizations. Those that come from the organizations with more status set the tone of the discussion about what is going on between the organizations. This is perhaps nowhere more clear than in donor–community organization relations, for there the donor is listened to about what has transpired between the groups.

Increasingly, evaluations done by social scientists are the mechanism for establishing that moral hegemony. The evaluation states the position of the superordinate group vis-a–vis the subordinate group. It establishes the criteria for the judgment and often it is the judgment about how well the subordinate group did its job.

The questions superordinate groups ask reflect their interests and purposes. These tend to underestimate the politics of groups receiving the funding. The result is an evaluation technology that downplays the local knowledge of the reform and homogenizes these efforts.

Most of us who do social science for a living accept this situation. The scientific assessment of behavior is usually seen as positive because it is the most unbiased and fair way to decide how well the actors have performed. Indeed we have been socialized and educated throughout our professional lives to believe that this hierarchy is the way things ought to be.

The problem with this state of affairs is that we have lost sight of the interactional realities of reform. First, we lose the perspective of the subordinate organizations and the meanings they attach to the behavior they are engaged in and second we may not understand correctly what has transpired because we have only a partial view of a political situation. In this book we attempted to ameliorate the situation by listening carefully to those who are situated in the subordinate position and show how what they think and do affects the outcomes that are of interest to the superordinates. This means taking seriously the specific situations that we are studying, for the actions of the subordinate groups are derivative of the local context. It means seeing the situation from their point of view and showing how that view affects what is happening. This does not in and of itself mitigate the questions and issues of the other groups but it does show how the interaction between the groups accounts for what transpires. If we only ask questions that represent the superordinate's perspective we may, for the sake of perpetuating the hierarchy, misunderstand what has transpired between the organizations involved.

# Appendix:
# Methodology

## Research Design

The basic research design used in chapter 7 is what Cook and Campbell (1979) call the "Untreated Control Group Design with Pretest and Posttest." That is, measurement was taken before and after the implementation of the crime prevention program in the "treated" neighborhoods, and identical measurement occurred at the same time in "untreated" (comparison) neighborhoods, as well as a citywide sample of Chicago residents. A one-year lag was scheduled between the pretest and the posttest, with most of the quantitative data collected in February and March of 1983 and again in 1984. Field work was continued throughout the implementation period.

### Types of Samples

Two types of samples were employed in this evaluation: panel samples and independent samples. While a panel design (with proper control groups) is generally stronger than the independent samples design on "internal validity" (i.e., the extent to which allows a strong inference that x caused y), the reverse is likely to be true with regard to "external validity" (i.e., the extent to which the results can be generalized to other settings, populations, etc.). The primary thrust of the evaluation was to assess the impact of these programs on neighborhood residents over a one–year time period. A panel design, involving repeated measurement on the *same* respondents over time, provided the strongest test of the "individual change" hypothesis. Error variance was reduced as each respondent served as his/her own control. Thus the panel data were given special attention in this evaluation.

## Selecting Treated and Untreated Neighborhoods

### Treated Neighborhoods

We selected only five of the ten funded organizations for inclusion in the evaluation to maintain a high quality evaluation given the resources available. Our influence over the selection of treatment neighborhoods *within* the five chosen community areas was limited to setting two restrictions on the community organizations making these decisions: (1) the programs should be implemented in neighborhoods where their organization had not carried out any community organizing in the past two years, especially crime prevention activities, and (2) the programs should be implemented in contiguous areas whenever possible. These requests were respected by three of the five community organizations. Only four of the five selected organizations were able to mount some type of crime prevention program during the timeframe of the evaluation.

*Untreated Comparison Neighborhoods*

As noted earlier, the research design called for two primary types of control groups: (1) untreated comparison neighborhoods that are similar to the treated neighborhoods on some basic characteristics, and (2) a city-wide comparison group that would not be vulnerable to local history and should detect citywide changes. To avoid the shortcomings of using a single location as a comparison neighborhood, we decided to use a pooled control group that would contain data from three separate locations within the city. We reasoned that this strategy would provide more stability and robustness to the findings. (For a detailed description of the selection process, see Rosenbaum et al, 1985.)

## Data Collection Methods and Procedures

Several sources of data and methodologies were employed in this project. The primary methodologies were telephone surveys of neighborhood residents, field work focused on participant observations, interviews with community organization leaders and staff, and reviews of written materials. The telephone surveys generated the data needed to assess changes in residents' perceptions, attitudes, feelings, and behaviors over time, thus allowing us to determine the extent and nature of program impact. In the context of impact assessment, the field work results were used to assist in the planning of survey analyses and the interpretation of survey results.

*Sampling Strategy*

In the absence of prior knowledge about whether the crime prevention activities would be implemented at the block or neighborhood level, a multi–level sampling scheme was used. Blockfaces (i.e., adjacent sides of two city blocks that share the same street) were randomly selected to represent neighborhood areas and then households were randomly selected to represent each of these selected blockfaces. The central hypothesis suggests that community crime prevention interventions can produce benefits for both participants and nonparticipants who live in the same "treated" areas. Consequently, our sample was not limited to participants.

With emphasis on measuring change in small geographic areas, rather than estimating population parameters, our main sampling frame was the list of published telephone numbers in these target areas. However, a random–digit–dial (RDD) telephone survey was used to generate a citywide control group.

The last defining characteristic of our sampling plan was the method of respondent selection. For all telephone surveys (both RDD and directory-based) the head–of–household selection technique was used.

*Completion Rates and Sample Sizes*

At Time 1, a total of 3357 interviews were completed. There were 1746 "refusals" of various types, thus yielding a completion rate of 65.8 percent. At Time 2, 1657 respondents were reinterviewed from the original sample, hence creating the panel sample. In addition, 1172 new "posttest only" residents were interviewed, bringing the total Time 2 sample to 2824. There were 1301 refusals at Time 2 (including over 500 respondents who had moved since Time 1), thus producing a completion rate of 68.0 percent.

*Measurement*

The survey instrument contained more than 200 items measuring a variety of constructs. A careful attempt was made to incorporate "proven" items from previous research on reaction to crime and fear of crime. Instruments from several major studies were reviewed and different measures were compared. In addition to building upon earlier research we expanded the scope of measurement to include variables in such areas as perceived efficacy.

Multi–item scales were developed (through factor analysis and reliability analysis) to measure a broad range of theoretical constructs pertinent to the main hypotheses. In total twenty–three separate scales were used to assess both the extent of program implementation and intermediate program effects on a wide variety of perceptions, emotions, attitudes, and behaviors.

# References

Alford, R.R. and R. Friedland. "Political Participation and Public Policy," *Political Participation* (1975).

Alinsky, S. *Reveille for Radicals.* New York: Vintage Books (1946).

Banfield, E.C. and J.Q. Wilson. *City Politics.* New York: Vintage Books (1963).

Baumer, T.L. and D.P. Rosenbaum. *Measuring Fear of Crime.* A Final Report Submitted to the National Institute of Justice, U.S. Department of Justice. Evanston, IL: Westinghouse Evaluation Institute (1981).

Becker, H.S. *Outsiders: Studies in the Sociology of Deviance.* New York: The Free Press (1963).

Becker, H.S. "Whose Side Are We On?" *Social Problems* 14 (Winter 1967):239–247.

Becker, H.S. "Culture: A Sociological View," *The Yale Review* (Summer 1982):513–527.

Blumer, H. "Social Problems as Collective Behavior," *Social Problems* 18 (1971):298–306.

Brown, R.H. "Bureaucracy as Praxis: Toward a Political Phenomenology of Formal Organizations," *Administrative Science Quarterly* 23 (1978):365–382.

Burgess, E.W., J. Lohman and C. Shaw. "The Chicago Area Project," *Coping with Crime.* New York: Yearbook of the National Probation Association (1937).

Carey, J.T. *Sociolog and Public Affairs: The Chicago School.* London: Sage Publications (1975).

Chicago Alliance for Neighborhood Safety. *Block Watch Organizing Handbook.* Chicago (1985).

Chicago Fact Book Consortium (eds.). *Local Community Fact Book Chicago Metropolitan Area.* Chicago: The Chicago Review Press (1984).

Citizen Information Service of Illinois. *Community–Directed Crime Prevention: An Alternative That Works.* Final Report to the National Institute of Justice. Chicago: Citizen Information Service of Illinois (1982).

Cloward, R. and L. Ohlin. *Delinquency and Opportunity: A Theory of Delinquent Gangs.* Glencoe, IL: Free Press (1960).

Cloward, R. and F. Piven. *The Politics of Turmoil.* New York: Pantheon Books (1974).

Cohen, S. *Visions of Social Control: Crime, Punishment, and Classification.* New York: Basil Blackwell, Inc. (1985).

Conklin, J.E. *The Impact of Crime.* New York: MacMillan Co. (1975).

Cook, F.L. "Crime and the Elderly: The Emergence of a Policy Issue," in D.A. Lewis (ed.) *Reactions to Crime.* Beverly Hills, CA: Sage Publications (1981).

Cook, T.D. and D.T. Campbell. *Quasi–Experimentation: Design and Analysis Issues for Field Settings.* Chicago: Rand McNally (1979).

Elmore, R.F. "Backward Mapping: Implementation Research and Policy Decisions," *Political Science Quarterly* 94, 4 (1979–80):601–616.

Fish, J. *Black Power/White Control: The Struggle of the Woodlawn Organization in Chicago.* Princeton, NJ: Princeton University Press (1973).

Frank, A.G. *Dependent Accumulation and Underdevelopment.* New York: Monthly Review Press (1979).

Gallup, G.H. *The Gallup Report #200.* Princeton, NJ: Gallup Poll (1981):22–23.

Garofalo, J. and M. McLeod. "A National Overview of the Neighborhood Watch Program." Paper presented at the Annual Meeting of the American Society of Criminology, San Diego (November 1985).

Giamartino, G.A. and A. Wandersman. "Organizational Climate Correlates of Viable Urban Block Organizations," *American Journal of Community Psychology* 11, 5 (1983):529–541.

Gittell, M. *Limits to Citizen Participation.* Beverly Hills, CA: Sage Publications (1980).

Gouldner, A.W. "The Sociologist as Partisan: Sociology and the Welfare State," *The American Sociologist* 2–3 (1968):103–116.

Granovetter, M.S. "The Strength of Weak Ties," *American Journal of Sociology* 78, 6 (1973):1360–1380.

Greenberg, S.W., W.M. Rohe and J.R. Williams. *Informal Citizen Action and Crime Prevention at the Neighborhood Level.* Washington, DC: Government Printing Office (1985).

Greenstone, J.D. and P.E. Peterson. *Race and Authority in Urban Politics.* New York: Russell Sage Foundation (1973).

Grimshaw, W.J. "Is Chicago Ready for Reform? A New Agenda for Harold Washington," *The Making of the Mayor* (n.d.).

Haveman, R.H. *A Decade of Federal Antipoverty Programs: Achievements, Failures, and Lessons.* New York: Academic Press (1977).

Heclo, H. "Two Traditions of General Welfare," *Political Science Quarterly* 101, 2 (1986):179–196.

Helfgot, J. "Professional Reform Organizations and the Symbolic Representation of the Pool," *American Sociological Review* 39, 4 (1974):475–491.

Hirschman, A.O. *Exit, Voice and Loyalty: Responses to Decline in Firms, Organization, and States.* Cambridge, MA: Harvard University Press (1970).

Jacobs, J. *The Death and Life of Great American Cities.* New York: Vintage (1961).

Katznelson, I. *Black Men, White Cities: Race, Politics, and Migration in the United States, 1900–1930, and Britain, 1948–1968.* Chicago: The University of Chicago Press (1973).

Kinsey, R., J. Lea and J. Young. *Losing the Fight Against Crime.* New York: Basil Blackwell, Inc. (1986).

Kohfeld, C.W., B. Salert and S. Schoenberg. "The Impact of Neighborhood Associations on Urban Crime Rates." Prepared for presentation at the Annual Meeting of the Western Political Science Association (March 1980).

Kornhauser, W. *The Politics of Mass Society.* New York: Free Press (1959).

Levy, F.S., et al. *Urban Outcomes.* Berkeley, CA: University of California Press (1974).

Lewis, D.A. "Design Problems in Public Policy Development." *Criminology* 17, 2 (1979):172–183.

Lewis, D.A. and M. Fenster. "Crime, Class and Community Organizations: A Replication of the Gittell Hypothesis." Presented at Law and Society Annual Meeting (1981).

Lewis, D.A. and G. Salem. "Community Crime Prevention: An Analysis of a Developing Strategy," *Crime and Delinquency* (July 1981):405–421.

Lipsky, M. *Protest in City Politics: Rent Strikes, Housing and the Power of the Poor.* Chicago: Rand McNally (1970).

Lipsky, M. and M. Levi. "Community as a Political Resource," in H. Hahn (ed.) *People and Politics in Urban Society.* Vol. 6 of *Urban Affairs Annual Reviews.* Beverly Hills, CA: Sage Publications (1972).

Lofland, L.H. "Understanding Urban Life: The Chicago Legacy," *Urban Life* 11, 4 (1983):491–511.

Lukes, S. *Essays in Social Theory.* New York: Columbia University Press (1977).

Marris, P. and M. Rein. *Dilemmas of Social Reform.* New York: Athenton Press (1967).

Merton, R.K. "Social Structure and Anomie," *American Sociological Review* 3 (1938):672–682.

Milbrath, L. and M.L. Goel. *Political Participation: How and Why Do People Get Involved in Politics.* (2nd ed.) Chicago: Rand McNally (1977).

Miliband, R. *The State in Capitalistic Society.* New York: Basic Books (1969).

Moe, T.M. "A Calculus of Group Membership," *American Journal of Political Science,* 24, 4 (1980).

Moe, T.M. "Toward A Broader View of Interest Groups," *The Journal of Politics* 43 (1981).

Mollenkopf, J. "Neighborhood Political Development and the Politics of Urban Growth: Boston and San Francisco, 1958–1978," *International Journal of Urban and Regional Research* 5, 1 (1981):15–39.

Molotch, H. "Capital and Neighborhood in the USA," *Urban Affairs Quarterly* 14, 3 (1979):289–312.

Moynihan, D.P. "The Professionalization of Reform," *The Public Interest* 1 (1965):6–16.

Olson, M. *The Logic of Collective Action: Public Goods and the Theory of Groups.* Cambridge, MA: Harvard University Press (1965).

Park, R.E. "Human Nature and Collective Behavior," *The American Journal of Sociology* 32 (1927):733–741.

Park, R.E. "Sociology and the Social Sciences: The Group Concept and Social Research," *The American Journal of Sociology* 27, 2 (1921):169–183.

Park, R.E., E.W. Burgess and R.D. McKenzie. *The City.* Chicago: University of Chicago Press (1925, republished in 1970).

Piven, F. "Deviant Behavior and the Remaking of the World," *Social Problems* 28, 5 (1981):489–508.

Piven, F. and R.A. Cloward. *Poor People's Movements.* New York: Vintage Books (1977).

Piven, F. and R.A. Cloward. *Regulating the Poor.* New York: Vintage Books (1971).

Podolefsky, A.M. "Rejecting Crime Prevention Programs: The Dynamics of Program Implementation in High Need Communities," *Human Organization,* 44, 1 (1985):33–40.

Pollock, P.H. III. "Organizations as Agents of Mobilization: How Does Group Activity Affect Political Participation?" *American Journal of Political Science* 26, 3 (1982).

Poulantzas, N. "The Problem of the Capitalistic State," in Robin Blackburn (ed.) *Ideology in Social Science.* New York: Vintage Books (1973).

Rainwater, L. "The Problem of Lower–Class Culture and Poverty–War Strategy," in D.P. Moynihan (ed.) *On Understanding Poverty: Perspectives from the Social Sciences.* New York: Basic Books (1969).

Rainwater, L. *What Money Buys.* New York: Basic Books (1974).

Reynolds, H.T. *Analysis of Nominal Data.* Beverly Hills, CA: Sage Publications (1977).

Rich, R. "A Political Economy Approach to the Study of Neighborhood Organizations," *American Journal of Political Science* 24 (1980):559–592.

Rosenbaum, D.P. (ed.). *Community Crime Prevention: Does It Work?* Beverly Hills, CA: Sage Publications (1986).

Rosenbaum, D.P. "The Theory and Research Behind Neighborhood Watch: Is It a Sound Fear and Crime Reduction Strategy?" *Crime and Delinquency* 33 (1987):103–134.

Rosenbaum, D.P., D.A. Lewis and J.A. Grant. *The Impact of Community Crime Prevention Programs in Chicago: Can Neighborhood Organizations Make a Difference?* Final Report Vol. 1 to the Ford Foundation. Evanston, IL: Center for Urban Affairs and Policy Research, Northwestern University (1985).

Rosenbaum, D.P., D.A. Lewis and J.A. Grant. "Neighborhood–Based Crime Prevention: Assessing the Efficacy of Community Organizing in Chicago," in D.P. Rosenbaum (ed.) *Community Crime Prevention: Does It Work?* Beverly Hills, CA: Sage Publications (1986).

Saunders, P. *Under Politics: A Sociological Interpretation.* London: Hutchinson (1979).

Schlossman, S. and M. Sedlak. "The Chicago Area Project Revisited," *Crime and Delinquency* 29, 3 (1983):398–462.

Seattle Police Department. *Citizen's Guide to Organizing a Block Watch.* Seattle, WA: City of Seattle (n.d.).

Shaw, C.R. and H.D. McKay. *Juvenile Delinquency and Urban Areas.* Chicago: University of Chicago Press (1942).

Shaw, C.R., F. Zorbaugh, H.D. McKay and L.S. Cottrell. *Delinquency Areas.* Chicago: University of Chicago Press (1929).

Skocpol, T. "Political Response to Capitalist Crisis: Neo–Marxist Theories of the State and the Case of the New Deal," *Politics and Society* 10 (1980):155–201.

Skogan, W.G. and M.G. Maxfield. *Coping with Crime.* Beverly Hills, CA: Sage Publications (1981).

Smith, M.P. *The City and Social Theory.* New York: St. Martins Press (1979).

Snodgrass, J. "Clifford R. Shaw and Henry D. McKay: Chicago Criminologists," *British Journal of Criminology* 16 (1976):1–19.

Tannenbaum, F. *Crime and the Community.* Boston: Ginn and Co. (1938).

Taub, R.P., D.G. Taylor and J.D. Dunham. *Paths of Neighborhood Change.* Chicago: University of Chicago Press (1984).

Taylor, I., P. Walton and J. Young. *The New Criminology: For a Social Theory of Deviance.* New York: Harper and Row (1973).

Thomas, W.I. and F. Znaniecki. *The Polish Peasant in Europe and America.* New York: Social Science Research Council (1939).

Unger, D.G. and A. Wandersman. "The Importance of Neighbors: The Social, Cognitive, and Affective Components of Neighboring," *American Journal of Community Psychology* 13, 2 (1985):139–169.

Verba, S. and N. Nie. *Participation in America: Political Democracy and Social Equality.* New York: Harper and Row (1972).

Wallerstein, I. *The Capitalist World–Economy.* Cambridge: Cambridge University Press (1979).

Weatherly, R.A. *Reforming Special Education: Policy Implementation from State Level to Street Level.* Cambridge, MA: MIT Press (1979).

Weissman, H.H. (ed.). *Community Development: In the Mobilization for Youth Experience.* New York: Association Press (1969).

Wilson, J.Q. *Political Organizations.* New York: Basic Books (1973).

Wilson, J.Q. and R. Herrnstein. *Crime and Human Nature.* New York: Simon and Schuster (1985).

Wirth, L. "The Scope and Problems of the Community," in Albert J. Reiss (ed.) *On Cities and Social Life.* Chicago: University of Chicago Press (1933).

Wirth, L. "Urbanism as a Way of Life," *American Journal of Sociology* 44, 1 (1938):1–4.

Wright, E.O. *Class, Crisis and the State.* London: Verso Editions (1979).

Yin, R.K. *What Is Citizen Crime Prevention? How Well Does It Work? Review of Criminal Justice Evaluation, 1978.* Washington, DC: U.S. Department of Justice Law Enforcement Administration, National Institute of Law Enforcement and Criminal Justice (1979).

# Index